RALPH STORER is an experienced hillwalker who has hiked extensively around the world. Despite being a Sassenach by birth, he has
lived in Scotland since studying psychology at Dundee University
and has a great affinity for the Highlands. As well as disappearing
into the hills for a regular fix of nature, he also writes novels and
sexological non-fiction, and produces darkwave music on his home
computer.

By the same author:

100 Best Routes on Scottish Mountains (Warner Books, 2013)

50 Best Routes on Skye and Raasay (Birlinn, 2012)

Exploring Scottish Hill Tracks: An Illustrated Route Guide for Walkers and Mountain Bikers (Warner Books, 1998)

The Joy of Hillwalking (Luath Press, 2004)

Mountain Trivia Challenge (Menasha Ridge Press, 1995)

The Rumpy Pumpy Quiz Book (Metro Publishing, 2003)

Love Scenes (a novel) (Mercat Press, 2004)

50 Classic Routes on Scottish Mountains (Luath Press, 2005)

The Ultimate Guide to the Munros, Volume 1: The Southern Highlands (Luath Press, 2014)

The Ultimate Guide to the Munros, Volume 2: Central Highlands South (Luath Press, 2011)

The Ultimate Guide to the Munros, Volume 3: Central Highlands North (Luath Press, 2011)

The Ultimate Guide to the Munros, Volume 4: Cairngorms South (Luath Press, 2012)

Baffies' Easy Munro Guide, Volume 1: Southern Highlands (Luath Press, 2012)

Baffies' Easy Munro Guide, Volume 2: Central Highlands (Luath Press, 2012)

The Ultimate Mountain Trivia Quiz Challenge (Luath Press, 2013)

50

Shades of Hillwalking

RALPH STORER

Luath Press Limited
EDINBURGH
www.luath.co.uk

First published 2014

ISBN: 978-1-910021-65-1

The paper used in this book is recyclable. It is made from
low chlorine pulps produced in a low energy, low emission manner
from renewable forests.

Printed and bound by
Bell & Bain Ltd., Glasgow

Typeset in 9.5 point Sabon and Frutiger

Versions of 32 have previously appeared in *TGO* magazine,
39 in *The Scotsman* newspaper, 40 in *The Herald* newspaper,
46 and 49 in *Country Walking* magazine,
and 50 in *The Angry Corrie*.

Contents

Siren Call

1	An Eerie Moan	9
2	A Bump Too Far	12
3	Roaming Free	14
4	Odyssey	17
5	The Long Hot Summer of Love	19
6	Cracked Alpinist	22
7	High Plains Drifter	27

Awesome Adventures

8	A Lad in Seyne	30
9	A Peripatetic Highpoint	34
10	Bottoming the Inverted Mountain	37
11	The Big One in One Day	42
12	In the Wake of the Gold Rush	46
13	Excelsior Among the Barkeaters	51
14	3,000m High in the Indian Ocean	55

Eccentric Escapades

15	Coasteering on Skye	61
16	Nutty Deals a Face Plant	65
17	Into Cairngorms Backcountry	68
18	Above the Great Salt Lake	71
19	Red Faces on the Canyon Rim	74
20	Canyoneering in Utah	78
21	Tatraneering for All	81

Misguided Misadventures

22	Blood Trails of Greece	87
23	Seconds Away	90
24	Going Underground	93
25	The Plughole Extension	97
26	Snowbound in Wartime	100
27	Icefall Shenanigans	103
28	Hooves from Hell	107

Pointless Pursuits

29	Ben Neverest	110
30	The Tri-Country Day Hike	113
31	The King of All Ben Lomonds	115
32	Sand Mountaineering	119
33	Brollibond or Bust	122
34	Highpointers and Peakbaggers	125
35	The Lost Art of Festering	129

Devil's Advocate

36	Blowing Hot and Cold	134
37	Leave No Trace	136
38	A Mountain by Any Other Name	139
39	The Chain Gang	143
40	A Summit For All	146
41	Ribbons of Stone	150
42	The Psychology of Risk	155

Carpe Diem

43	Bothy Extracts	159
44	Hiking in Clan and Tribal Country	163
45	The Wisdom of Chief Joseph	167
46	Munro Bagging with Queen Victoria	170
47	Lost Innocence	174
48	I Keep the Dreams	177
49	Hillwalking Saved My Life	179
50	A Politically Correct Hillwalking Fable	183

Siren Call

1

An Eerie Moan

I BLAME THE music master, but not because he nearly killed me. If it wasn't for him, I might not have discovered mountains when it mattered. I was an east coast boy. I reached my teenage years without ever having seen a hill higher than a Lincolnshire Wold.

I don't know why a music teacher with no leadership skills or qualifications would decide (or be allowed) to take a bunch of spotty adolescent schoolboys up Snowdon in the middle of February. Even more puzzling, I don't know why Dave and I would decide to join his little group. Or why my parents would fork out the princely sum of £14 to cover the week's train, coach and living expenses, and equip me with boots, anorak and over-trousers from the Army and Navy Stores.

Yet, in the winter of 1961, Dave and I and the music master and several schoolmates set out from Llanberis Youth Hostel to climb the path beside the Snowdon railway. We had no ice axes or crampons. I wouldn't even have known what these were. In any case, cloud obscured the summit and hid the snowbound upper slopes, which offered the prospect of an once-in-a-life-time slide down over the crags of Clogwyn du'r Arddu. We were blissfully unaware of the many accidents, some of them fatal, which had occurred here.

At Clogwyn Station we reached the base of the cloud and the first flush of snow, at which point the music master informed us that his boots were too worn to continue. Anyone who wished

Three came back... just (author in centre)

to climb the last 500 yards to the summit was at liberty to do so while the rest waited. Three of us took up the challenge – myself, Dave and a schoolmate from another class whose name I no longer remember.

Within a short distance the path disappeared, to be replaced by a smooth snow bank that angled up to our left and fell away into the mist on our right. Only a thin line of shallow footprints hinted at the route onwards. In our innocence, we sat on the snow bank, stamped our heels into the footprints and continued to inch summit-wards with crablike movements. My thin nylon anorak soon became a wet rag and my even thinner nylon over-trousers were ripped apart by the wind, but the swirling cloud made us unaware of the abyss below our feet and the danger we were in.

I still recall the moment that our schoolmate lost his footing and began to slide away from us. By chance, before he gathered speed, his boot caught on a protruding pebble and his flailing hands managed to indent the snow sufficiently to gain purchase. He gasped. Dave and I held our breath. We were good boys and didn't swear.

Somehow, the boy wormed his way back up beside us and the precariousness of our position finally dawned on us. We retreated, in earnest silence, with infinitely more caution than we

SIREN CALL

had ascended. At Clogwyn Station the music master and his party merely greeted us with impatience and set off down the path at a clip.

We three were unscathed but, as I descended, I began to lag behind. I clung gamely to my torn overtrousers, which blew out horizontally from my waist. My mother would surely be angry if I returned without them. She was a good knitter and could probably mend them. I was soaked to the skin and unable to stop shivering. Yet I seemed not to mind. On the contrary, I began to feel curiously light-headed. I now realise, of course, that I was suffering from incipient exposure.

The music master eventually noticed my sluggishness and waited for me to rejoin the group. I remember nothing of the remainder of the descent. In the following days we climbed other hills below the snowline, and I remember little of those too. Yet that experience on Snowdon has stayed with me over the years. In fact, for some reason, perhaps the same mysterious reason that makes others want to climb mountains too, it even whetted my appetite for more.

I arrived home to find my family bickering over the quickest way to get from one location in town to another. It was a not unusual scenario. Who cared? Didn't they know about mountains? I retired to my room. I was 14 years old, so I cried.

In those days the YHA produced small walking guides called log books. The Snowdon Log cost me two shillings (10p), a not inconsiderable chunk of pocket money, but I had to have it. It included a passage from H.V. Morton's book *In Search of Wales*, which both encapsulated my feelings and fired my imagination: 'The mist moved thickly and the wind came over the top of Snowdon to an eerie moan.'

I had heard that eerie moan. It was a siren call.

2

A Bump Too Far

THE GRASSY RIDGE curved down from summit to base in a single great arc, undulating over a series of bumps before fanning out steeply below a prominent shoulder. I eyed that shoulder greedily. It hung in the sky, perhaps 500ft above me. Surely there was time?

My family had stopped for lunch beside the stream that wound around the foot of the ridge. It was 12 o'clock. It was always 12 o'clock because my aunt had diabetes and needed sustenance at that time. For several years, a week's holiday in a caravan site in the Lake District was an annual ritual for my extended family.

Lunch would take at least an hour. My mother had yet to begin making the ham sandwiches. My father had yet to light the stove to boil the water for the tea. Younger relations had not yet decided where to start building their dam across the stream.

Having extracted permission to eat later, I was given freedom to roam, provided I returned within the hour. My professed aim was to take a photograph of the view from the shoulder, and I carried a Kodak Brownie 127 in support of the ruse, but my real aim was simply to reach the shoulder.

Of course, I set off too fast. I was an unfit teenager – school team sports had never appealed to me – and had yet to learn about pacing. Soon I was gasping for breath. Desire kept me going, as it has so often since. I needed to reach that shoulder.

When I did so, the feeling was more of relief than exultation. I collapsed on the ground until my heart rate returned to normal then took the obligatory photograph to justify my endeavour. My family were specks below me. The children were still in the stream. I looked upwards. The angle of the ridge lessened and the next bump seemed not so far away. I had no watch, but I couldn't have been away for half an hour yet. Surely there was time?

Prior exertions forgotten, I set off again. Too fast, again. Out of breath, again. I reached the bump. Perhaps half an hour had now passed and it was time to descend. But descent would be quicker. I could climb for 35 minutes, maybe 40, then bound down and still make it in an hour. The next bump seemed close at hand...

By the time I'd reached it, I had climbed maybe 1,000ft but was still not even halfway up the ridge. The next bump beckoned, and the one beyond that, and the summit higher still. But I realised now that my time was up. Reluctantly, I turned and galumphed back down with great loping strides.

I couldn't have been away for much more than my allotted hour but, by the time I reached the foot of the ridge, the stream was devoid of children, the picnic paraphernalia had been packed away and the family was ready to move on. I had kept them waiting. As I was too old for a clip round the ear to have any meaningful effect, I was subjected to verbal scalding for the remainder of the afternoon.

My family just didn't understand, I reasoned, and retreated into sullen silence, pining for the hill. No one understood how I felt. How could they? I was probably the first person in the history of the human race to experience such feelings.

How to explain the lure of the hills to those who don't feel it? I don't even understand it myself. I have spent my whole life going for that next bump, and not just on mountains. Sometimes, as on that family outing in the Lake District, it has been a selfish pursuit, but it is a part of who I am and I can make no apologies for it.

When experienced mountaineer Alison Hargreaves, the mother of two young children, was killed while descending from the summit of K2 in 1995, she was posthumously criticised for attempting such a risky venture. I too have lost friends who went for that next bump and never returned. But I cannot blame them. It was a part of who they were. What are we without desire, without ambition, without dreams?

3

Roaming Free

IN 1965 THE concept of a gap year between school and university did not exist. Going abroad at all, even across the Channel to France, was a distant dream. But Dave and I ached for adventure, and what could be more adventurous than spending a week in the Lake District crossing the hills from one youth hostel to another? It would be our first time away from home on our own, free of adult control. The very idea of it was enough to induce giddiness.

The only fixed points on our itinerary were Keswick station, where we would arrive and leave, and the three 3,000ft summits of Skiddaw, Helvellyn and Scafell Pike. As we possessed neither tent nor camping equipment, youth hostels provided the only food and lodging we could afford. We highlighted all of them on our one-inch-to-one-mile Ordnance Survey map and, throughout the winter of our last year in the sixth form, pored over route possibilities as though planning a Himalayan expedition. Sir John Hunt could have been no more thorough.

A summer spent freezing peas in a Humber Bank factory provided funds and we detrained in Keswick scarcely able to believe that our plans had come to fruition. Robert Louis Stevenson wrote that 'to travel hopefully is a better thing than to arrive' but he might have changed his mind had he seen Dave and I standing wide-eyed on Keswick station platform.

On our first day we climbed Skiddaw, using Poucher's *Lakeland Peaks* as a guide. I remember nothing of the ascent but, according to the diary I kept of the trip, we encountered cloud, rain, bog and river crossings. Apparently, we thought it a good idea to make do with one rucksack and take it in turns to carry it. It was an experiment we chose not to repeat. Yet still I managed to note in my diary, heavily influenced by Poucher's

Looking cool on Striding Edge

ornate prose, that Back o' Skiddaw was 'a paradise of wilderness where a man can finally be as free as nature intended him to be'.

In the ensuing week, no matter how often it rained or how many times we lost our way, we kept strictly to our planned itinerary. We had to. We'd pre-booked every hostel so we had to reach each by 7pm or miss a dinner for which we'd already paid.

From Keswick we crossed the hills to Helvellyn and descended Striding Edge. My diary informs me that 'such grandeur we had never seen before'. The following day we climbed Helvellyn again by Swirral Edge and descended to Grasmere. After that we worked our way down to Coniston Old Man and back over Scafell Pike before returning to Keswick via Borrowdale.

I wish I could recall it all more clearly, but the details are lost to memory. When I look at my diary now, it could have been written by a stranger. I find it hard to believe, for example, that we lost our way simply trying to get out of Keswick, or that for lunch I carried a packet of Sugar Frosties, a bar of Aero and a carton of Ribena.

The only hostel I remember is Coniston Coppermines, then a bleak, rarely visited building 500ft up the hillside, run by a big bearded bear of a man. He hadn't eaten hot food for a week and was glad of our arrival so that he could cook a basic meal for the three of us. There was a lot of cabbage. When we left the following morning, he called after us heartily: 'The next time you're passing... just keep passing.' It became a mantra that kept us going when energy lapsed.

My diary records one forgotten incident when I nearly lost my Wainwright guide to the Southern Fells (from his still unfinished Lakeland series). It fell out of my too-small anorak pocket and tumbled down a steep hillside into the confines of Tilberthwaite Ghyll on Wetherlam. At a cost of 15 shillings (75p), it was far too precious a purchase to abandon, so I made a hair-raising scramble down steep grass, retrieved it and carefully wiped each page clean as best I could. This incident must have occurred, because I still have that guidebook; it still falls open at Wetherlam and its pages are still a muddy brown.

Such details have faded with time, but what I shall never forget is the heady freedom I discovered in the hills that week. It is a feeling that has stayed with me in the years since, has lured me back to the hills time and time again, and is rekindled even as I write these words now. Fittingly, my diary of my week in the Lakes ends with a stunned revelation: 'I am at home here.'

4

Odyssey

'IT'S NOT BEAUTIFUL,' said Tony, 'but it's impressive.' Who was I to disagree? He was President of Dundee University Rucksack Club, while I was a mere bejant (the Dundee Uni equivalent of fresher). For me, he was a man whose every pronouncement bore the stamp of unimpeachable authority. But for once he was only half-right. As the Rucksack Club coach approached the head of Glen Coe, I wondered how anyone could not find the prospect beautiful.

The whole journey across the breadth of the country, from Dundee on the east coast to Glen Coe on the west, was a revelation to a geographically impoverished Sassenach. We passed lochs larger than anything I could have imagined. Loch Earn and Loch Tay alone could have swallowed all the Cumbrian lakes between them. Surely the Great Lakes of America could be no bigger?

Eager to assimilate as much of the experience as possible, I immediately resolved to pronounce these lochs like a local, and not as 'locks', like so many lazy Sassenachs. Such astonishing expanses of water, wild and forbidding, deserved no less. And I learned that the term Sassenach applied to all lowlanders, not just the English.

And the mountains! Instead of the handful of 3,000ft peaks I'd seen in Wales and the Lake District, this country had dozens, lined up in dazzling array as our cross-country road trip progressed. First up was pudding-like Ben Vorlich, which the old hands (i.e. second years and above) said hid a craggier and even more exciting peak called Stuc a' Chroin. Why aren't we climbing that, then, I wondered?

As we descended into Glen Dochart, my colleagues-to-be searched for a glimpse of Ben Lawers and Meall nan Tarm-

The Rucksack Club coach at Ben Lawers

achan. I made mental notes as they reminisced about their exploits on the high summit ridges. Soon pyramid-like Ben More dominated the view ahead, then twin-peaked Ben Lui with its Central Gully, then the soaring arrowhead of Ben Dorain. It was all too much to take in. How could anyone remember the names of all these mountains, let alone discuss them as though they were old friends? And I learned that there weren't just dozens, there were hundreds, and for some reason they were called Munros. It was enough to boggle the mind.

Finally we reached Glen Coe, the annual destination for the inaugural Rucksack Club meet of the academic year. Hemmed in by rocky peaks, what better place could there be to initiate first years into hillwalking in Scotland? Buachaille Etive Mor, Bidean nam Bian, Aonach Eagach... the strange Gaelic names tripped off Tony's tongue like secret passwords to a hidden kingdom. I immediately resolved to learn the ancient language of my new home.

There were maybe 30 of us on the coach. Tony divided us into parties of five or six, each led by an experienced leader. I joined his group on the traverse of Aonach Eagach. I didn't

SIREN CALL

know then of its fearsome reputation, but was told that if I'd managed Striding Edge on Helvellyn, I should be okay.

That first Scottish hill walk was one of the most exciting I have ever done. Everything about it was wonderful: the anticipation, the rock manoeuvres, the precarious situations, the views, the camaraderie... I descended to the glen desperate for more, as impatient for the following weekend's meet as a child for Christmas.

A few years later I became President of the Rucksack Club myself. Now it was my turn to introduce fresh-faced bejants and bejantines to the Highlands. Their wide-eyed fervour brought back memories of my own, while my new-found knowledge of the peaks impressed them as much as Tony's had impressed me. I envied the newcomers the discoveries that awaited them, but no more than they envied me.

Later still I would write guidebooks to the Scottish mountains and my initial awe would become tempered by fond familiarity. But even today, en route to some well-trodden summit, with nothing to distract from the steady footfall of boot on easy trail, something unexpected can still catch me unawares: a glimpse of a peak through a gap in the clouds, a previously unnoticed route variation, an ascent line metamorphosed by snow, a solitary orchid or dotterel. And I feel again, as though all experience counts for nothing, the fledgling's frisson of excitement.

5

The Long Hot Summer of Love

IN THE 1960s the first date pencilled in the calendar of Dundee University Rucksack Club was the end-of-year meet on the Isle

Home from the hill

of Skye. The establishment of a base camp in Glen Brittle after finals, shared with a number of other universities, was an annual and much anticipated ritual. From June to July, a core of Cuillin stalwarts would live here while others came and went as time allowed. This set-up produced an ever-changing series of climbing partners and a steady supply of experienced leaders to guide beginners up mountains that were still poorly mapped and described in guidebooks.

The Summer of '67 was blisteringly hot on Skye, and there is no heat like Cuillin heat. The range's great rock walls reflect and channel the sun's rays into the high corries, where the trapped heat bakes aspiring walkers and climbers in shimmering air. Throughout that glorious summer, while hippies indulged in love-ins and be-ins in San Francisco with flowers in their hair, we revelled in our climb-in in Glen Brittle with boots on our feet.

Each morning we were forced out of our tents by the glaring sun to see beckoning rock peaks piercing infinite blue skies. Still groggy from the previous day's exertions, we would mooch around camp and often not set off up the hill until after midday. This was not the result of laziness, but of the diurnal cycle into which, far from the time dictates of urban routine, we invariably slipped.

We would climb to the skyline and remain on one summit or another for the 11pm sunset show, whose seascapes and cloud-scapes were more colourful than I have seen anywhere. Only then would we head glenwards in the dying light for a campsite feast in the wee small hours before turning in.

Starting in the afternoon meant climbing during the hottest part of the day, but that was the way it was. Cascading streams and enticing lochans provided unsurpassable skinny dipping opportunities, while waterfalls formed grottos where colourful dragonflies filled the air in homage to a South Sea paradise. But always the summits were our goal.

After several such halcyon days on the heights, we became so blissfully 'dazed and confused' that we ached for a day of rain, or even a build-up of cloud in the corries, as an excuse for a spot of R&R. Sometimes we would repair to Sligachan Hotel for an evening of liquid refreshment. In those days the bar closed at 10pm, which gave time for a late night intervarsity football match back on Glen Brittle beach.

At other times a trip to Portree became necessary in order to restock food supplies. Campground facilities bordered on non-existent. There was no campground shop. A van would appear occasionally to sell the odd krab or tin of beans. Toilets and cold showers were housed in a Spartan brickhouse whose plumbing aspired to nothing more sumptuous than intermittent functionality.

It was in Portree that we came closest to the hippy Summer of Love for which the year was to become famous. In a now long-forgotten coffee bar on the quayside, we fed the jukebox and eyed up Portree High School senior girls across formica-topped tables to the strains of 'Purple Haze' and 'A Whiter Shade of Pale'.

Given our state when we returned from Skye and saw ourselves in a mirror – sunburnt and windswept, bearded and bedraggled, torn and tattered, grazed and gouged by gabbro – the chances of us being allowed to participate in the sexual revolution were pretty slim anyway. But revolutionary matters could wait for the cosy nights of winter. A summer on Skye could not.

As Alexander Smith recounted in his 1880 book *A Summer in Skye*, even the poorest man returns from the island with 'a picture gallery in his memory which he would not exchange for the Louvre'.

In the Summer of '67, when everything seemed possible, we made our choice and never regretted it.

6

Cracked Alpinist

AFTER YEARS OF hillwalking in the UK, the Alps came as a shock. I knew they were big mountains but, naïve as ever, I'd never expected them to look *that* big. My partner Christine and I refused to be intimidated. After all, we were there because they were big. We wanted to grab some altitude.

If 3,000ft (914m) was the cut-off point for what was deemed to be a mountain in Scotland, we decided that 3,000m would serve as an Alpine equivalent. As in the UK, there are many excellent mountains below this threshold but, with the limited time available to us during a fortnight's summer holiday, 3,000ers were the challenge we set ourselves.

The traditional way to reach a high Alpine peak is from a refuge (hut) strategically placed within reach of the summit, but first you have to reach the hut and we were loath to use up an extra day of precious holiday time in order to do so. Instead, we would climb from valley to summit in a single day by setting off *really* early. A 2,000m ascent would be accomplished by a brisk 1,000m hike up to a refuge for breakfast, followed by a further 1,000m ascent to the summit after that.

In this manner, over several summers, we worked our way down the French Alps to the Riviera, climbing 3,000ers region by region as we went. Travel constraints and technical difficulty put many of the high peaks out of reach, but there remained more than enough to keep us happy.

Then one year we decided we needed to get even higher and climb a 4,000er, which raised a whole new set of problems. At high altitude, snow conditions have a far greater diurnal range than on British mountains. Frozen overnight snow thaws sufficiently during the day to cause rockfall. A refuge-based night-time start would be necessary. Altitude would also be a problem.

Above all, we would be limited by our moderate ability to manage roped snow and ice work. We weren't seasoned Alpinists. We were humble but ambitious hillwalkers. We needed a peak that more experienced mountaineers would dismiss as too easy. We found it in the Ecrins National Park.

At 4,102m, the Barre des Écrins towers over the two-mile long Glacier Blanc (White Glacier), beside which the Refuge des Écrins provides an overnight base. The Barre itself sports a difficult summit ridge that was beyond our capabilities but, next to it, across a shallow col, no more than a shoulder really, was the rounded top of the 4,015m Dôme de Neige des Écrins. Even the name appealed. The Snow Dome. And so it came to pass that, one morning in the summer of 1982, with a mixture of trepidation and excitement, Christine and I set off from our valley campsite near the village of Ailefroide to embark on the great adventure.

The first day involved a 700m ascent to the Refuge du Glacier Blanc followed by a further 500m ascent to the Refuge des Écrins. A good trail led to the first refuge, which marked the turnaround point for day hikers. Above here, the going became tougher as the trail climbed around the séracs (ice cliffs) that formed the snout of the Glacier Blanc. Then the trail took to the glacier itself. An almost level surface made for easy going, but the numerous crevasses that had to be jumped certainly kept the mind focussed.

It was hard to believe we were already above 3,000m, yet great peaks rose even higher all around us. With the valley and the crowds behind us, we were entering the silent realm of what an old guidebook called the *Abode of the Snows*. Only now did the scale and seriousness of what we were attempting truly begin to dawn on us.

The Refuge des Écrins was perched on a rock bluff above the glacier, giving a perfect view across to the wedge-shaped Barre and Dôme – a single mountain with two tops separated by the shallow col that was our first objective. The white wall of snow and ice that formed the north face, and which would be our ascent route, looked incredibly steep.

Our evening meal at the refuge consisted of multifarious dehydrated substances, rehydrated with hot water purchased from the hut guardian. Lights-out was at 9.30pm. We were allotted spaces in the '5.30 dorm', on a wide bunk bed alongside a motley crew of fellow climbers. It was hot and stuffy, the snoring was industrial and someone was sick, either from wine or altitude. The whole experience was so surreal that at one point Christine was overcome by a fit of the giggles.

Sleeping in such conditions was obviously a skill we did not possess, but in any case we were roused from our bed two hours early when the hardened Alpinists of the '3.30 dorm' turned the refuge into a noisy hive of activity. Sleepily, we forced down some breakfast and ventured outside into the freezing night air. Somewhere up there in the darkness was our summit. 3,000ft to go. No more than a Munro, we said with little conviction.

The snow trail made by earlier parties led across the glacier and made routefinding simple. We trudged along half-asleep, clinging to our ice axes, head torches picking out boot prints. Then the sun rose and the world transformed. The snow glowed pink then sparkled brilliant white. We became specks in a vast landscape from which all colour had been drained. Only an occasional black rock face broke the dazzling brightness. The Barre and Dôme appeared above us, mist playing around their summits.

At the foot of the north face, layers of clothes came off and sunglasses replaced torches. Like the parties in front of us, we donned crampons and roped up. Experienced Alpinists routinely move together on steep ground but, for extra protection, we

The Barre des Ecrins (*left*) and the Dôme de Neige (*right*)

moved one at a time from belay to belay. For further reassurance, I was using a short 50ft length of rope to keep Christine close. I would lead a rope length, thrust my ice axe into the snow and use it as a belay to bring her up, then use her ice axe as a belay while I led the next section.

In this manner, we made slow but insistent progress up the face. The slope was continuously steep and increasingly exposed. The trail threaded a way over crevasses and around séracs. Every step required concentration, balance, precision. We breathed hard in the thin air. Some of the crevasses required an extra burst of effort to launch oneself from the lower near side to the higher far side. For us, this was serious stuff.

The route climbed directly towards the Barre then cut diagonally right beneath the summit ridge towards the col between the foot of the ridge and the Dôme. By the time we reached this traverse, the snow was beginning to soften and slabs of ice, some of them dislodged by climbers on the ridge above, whizzed past us. Now I understood why helmets, which we didn't possess, were a good idea. Considering the altitude, we made surprisingly short work of that traverse.

All that separated us from the summit now was a short snow arête. And suddenly we were there. The mist that had hovered around the summit all morning cleared for a while to open up the view, as though the mountain gods realised we needed confirmation of where we were. It was indeed true. Somehow, we had done it. We were standing at the summit of an Alpine 4,000er.

The next day, we sat dazed in a café in Ailefroide, scarcely able to believe our success. But we had proof. Fortunately or otherwise, to dispel all doubt, the climb had bequeathed to us a memento. To avoid high-altitude sunburn, we had lathered all exposed skin with triple layers of sunscreen, but there was one part of our bodies that we had failed to realise needed even more protection: our lips. They were now as cracked and crevassed as the Glacier Blanc.

I cannot tell you how painful the next few days were. No ointment could soothe the sting. Talking was difficult through lips cemented into a pout. Smiling was agony. Eating solid food was impossible. All we could manage was soup, sucked through a straw.

But would we have swapped our achievement for relief? No chance. Tight-mouthed and pinched we may have looked, but inside we glowed like the sun-kissed morning snows, and next time we would know better. The more passers-by looked at us with pity, the more we bore our discomfort as a badge of honour. We pitied them back because they had not seen what we had seen. The pain would go. Memories of the Abode of the Snows would stay with us forever.

7

High Plains Drifter

IN 1990 I fell in love with Pinedale. A sleepy cow town on the high plains of Wyoming, it offered little more than a handful of motels and eateries to detain the occasional traveller passing through on US Highway 191. Its main claim to fame was that it lay further from a railroad than any other town in the USA. These days, there's the added attraction of the Museum of the Mountain Man, but the population remains resolutely under four figures.

Visitors who fetch up in Pinedale usually do so for one reason only – to explore the Wind River Range, a 110-mile spine of Alpine mountains named after the river that is in turn named after the wind that blows almost incessantly across the vast Wyoming landscape. East of town the high peaks hang on the horizon like a jagged frieze.

One million acres of designated wilderness. Twenty-three 'thirteeners' (mountains higher than 13,000ft/3,950m). Seven of the ten largest glaciers in the USA outside Alaska. More than 100 cirques. More than 1,300 lakes. Plus approach trails of a length and altitude (10,000ft/ 3,000m) that puts the range well out of day-hike reach, ensuring that it remains one of the American West's great unsung beauty spots. What better choice for a first trip to the Rocky Mountains?

Following in the footsteps of the fabled mountain men who trapped beaver here in the 19th century, I disappeared into the wildest recesses of the Winds for two weeks, traversing the range from south to north. I was by now a seasoned hiker, a veteran of numerous trips in the high mountains of the Alps and Pyrenees, but the scenery here was on the grand scale, unlike anything I had seen on this side of the Atlantic.

In the Cirque of the Towers, fantastic spires with exotic names such as Warbonnet, Watch Tower and Shark's Nose formed a semi-circle of teetering rock peaks around Lonesome Lake. Further north, the mile-long wall of Haystack Peak towered over Deep Lake, where sparkling waterslides tumbled over boilerplate slabs into alluring pools.

Further north still, the islands, headlands and sandy bays of Island Lake gave it the improbable appearance of an Aegean coastline. Behind it stretched Titcomb Basin, a great U-shaped trench lined by a ribbon of turquoise lakes beneath a horseshoe of serrated thirteeners. And so much more, until my diary ran out of superlatives to describe the spectacle. If this was just one small part of what the American West had to offer, I was hooked. 'My America, my new-found-land,' as John Donne wrote.

Fitter but skinnier, I resurfaced at a Pinedale motel to reacquaint myself with modern life's everyday luxuries: a soft bed, hot water, artificial light, non-dehydrated food... The neon-lit Wrangler Café, with its fries and pies, was a gastronomic heaven. The Sweet Tooth Saloon offered up a *smörgåsbord* of sugary delights. The local library was a treasure trove of historical works on pioneering Scots such as John Stuart and William Stewart.

For a few days I kicked back and recharged, my life on pause, content to roam the rustic boardwalks, gaze at the distant Wind River peaks and dream of simpler times when beaver was king. In trapping days, mountain men, Indians, traders and hangers-on would meet once a year at a temporary encampment called Rendezvous, where pelts were traded for liquor and supplies and the living was as wild as only it can be when men have spent a year in the wilderness. Rendezvous died out with the beaver trade a century and a half ago, but if you arrive in Pinedale on the second weekend in July, as I did, you may think you have been transported back in time.

Beside the river are pitched a couple of dozen tipis, expertly constructed from tapering lodgepole pine cocooned with taut canvas. A banner says 'Welcome to Rendezvous.' Tacos fry on a makeshift wood fire. Traders in fur and buckskin sit around chewing the fat and selling Native American artefacts, paintings and trinkets made from various parts of buffalo. There are

On the shores of Deep Lake

shooting and axe-throwing contests. Young girls in buckskin dresses run around joyfully.

No one seems to mind whether you purchase anything or not. This is a re-creation of a lost part of the Wild West and to be there with like-minded enthusiasts is enough. In the evening everyone sits around a huge log fire, chatting and watching the flames. Some play banjo or sing as the mood takes them. Perhaps they have indeed recaptured something that has been lost since the days of the mountain men.

The day after Rendezvous, I hitched a lift out of town on the back of a pick-up truck. Perhaps I'd seen too many Hollywood movies, but there was something indescribably romantic about speeding along the two-lane blacktop with the wind in my hair, the asphalt reeling out behind and the sawtooth Wind River skyline receding into the distance.

Awesome Adventures

8

A Lad In Seyne

SUMMER'S THE TIME to go to the Alps. Obviously. Clement weather, paths clear of snow, meadows bursting with wild-flowers... Instead, the spirit moved me to backpack across the Provence Alps in spring. Mistake.

It looked fine on the map. A reassuringly fat red line marked the GR6, one of France's *Grandes Randonnées* (long-distance trails), a 45-mile route that linked the towns of Sisteron and Seyne and climbed no higher than 2,000m. A springtime crossing would avoid the debilitating heat of a Provençal summer and, that close to the Mediterranean, winter snows would already have melted. Surely.

I began in Sisteron, a picturesque town situated on the banks of the River Durance beneath fluted cliffs towering 300m over-head. The GR6 headed for high country immediately with a 600m ascent over the shoulder of the 1,147m Rocher de la Baume. All first days are tough, but the trail did its best to ease the burden of a full pack by climbing in shallow zigzags through a scented pine forest on a carpet of pine needles. Provence in springtime. Good choice, I told myself.

Entrepierres gorge provided a congenial riverside pitch for a first night in the wilds, with a *source* of excellent water in an abandoned hamlet. Such ghost villages are a feature of the high country of Provence, the old habitations having been left to decay when the people migrated to the towns. They make for spooky campsites but, as the horizon swallowed up the sun and darkness descended, I was more than content with my lot.

Day two began with a more intimate section of trail that contoured across high farmland, where splashes of red and white paint waymarked the route. I still managed to miss the painter's handiwork and unwittingly discover some interesting variations to the *voie normale*, but I remained vigilant not to stray too far from the trail because water was scarce. Finding a *source*, usually a spring or well in the broken-down outbuildings of some long-abandoned dwelling, was like finding nectar.

Eventually the trail quit its contour line and plunged down wooded slopes to the scorched valley of Abros, where the old village was under restoration and I succumbed to a riverside siesta in the afternoon heat. The lost height was regained on a lazy 500m climb out of the other side of the valley to the Col de Mounis. This would have made a fine campsite, but it was necessary to climb still a few hundred metres higher to the parched open land called Le Désert in order to camp close to the only *source* in the area (thankfully signposted). It turned out to be no more than a trickle of water buried in the undergrowth, but it did the job.

Day three. So far, so good. But now the easy-going GR6 decided on a change of policy. Having lured its followers into a false sense of accomplishment by taking the line of least resistance around highpoints, it now attacked every peak in its path directly. It climbed up and down Mélan (1,708m), then up and down Guéren (1,880m), until it came face to face with the redoubtable 2,000m mountains of the Val Haut Crest, dominated by the bulk of Les Monges (2,115m).

I camped on the slopes of Les Monges at the Col de Clapouse. In summer it would have been an unbearably waterless spot, but trickles of snowmelt from above made an overnight springtime pitch possible. That snowmelt should have forewarned be about what lay ahead on the remainder of the route. The GR6 would bypass the summit of Les Monges itself but then take a directissima line *over* the three remaining 2,000m peaks.

On Day four, the first of the three summits, La Laupie (2,025m), came underfoot with surprising ease, giving no inkling of the difficulties to come. Then the ridge narrowed. The wind speed increased exponentially. And suddenly I entered a whole new world of whiteness.

It was as if the GR6 had deliberately saved up all its snow and dumped it here. It was so soft and deep that every step became a trial. It took an age to cross the shallow dip between La Laupie and Le Clot de Genoux (2,112m) and even longer to cross the deeper gap that barred the way to L'Oratoire (2,071m), the third and final 2,000m peak. And matters were about to get worse.

L'Oratoire is a fine mountain of classic pyramid shape whose traverse in summer conditions is purported to provide an easy and wonderfully airy walk. Under snow, without skis or snow-shoes, it presented a virtually impassable barrier. The white stuff did its utmost to show me the infinite variety of forms into which it was able to shapeshift. Deep marshmallow snow alternated with ridges of hard frozen snow, interspersed with bottomless snow topped by a hard crust that broke thigh-deep just as weight was about to be transferred from one foot to the other.

Sometimes both legs disappeared into their own snow holes and I found myself half-buried, waist deep, with my pack denting the snow behind. If this situation coincided with a particularly strong gust of wind, I was rocked back and forth like a punch-ball. Extricating myself from such a predicament was inordinately time-consuming. I had to remove the pack, climb out of the hole and re-shoulder the pack, only to take another step and have to repeat the process all over again.

Progress ground almost to a standstill. I could see the ridiculous side of it, but some choice expletives were nevertheless borne away on the spindrift. Hours passed before I finally crested the summit of L'Oratoire and, on easier ground, was able to roll down the far side until the snow was left behind.

At last, nothing now blocked the way to Seyne. But if I thought my problems were over, I was about to be rudely disillusioned. The route into town merited barely a sentence in the

The Val Haut Crest

guidebook. The last few miles merely followed an anticlimactic cart track. What the guidebook failed to mention was that after rain the track became a slough of ankle-deep mud. And it appeared to have been raining on a scale that would have given Noah pause for concern.

Even worse, it may not have been *all* mud. Cattle had also been given free rein to use the track. The noxious smell that assailed my nostrils added to my sense of unease as the glutinous concoction sucked at my boots. Farmers in flanking fields shook their heads in Gallic bemusement at the sight of yet another flustered foreigner adopting a ridiculous high-stepping gait in a forlorn attempt to avoid splashes.

I reached Seyne aching from the contortions demanded of the Val Haut Crest and caked with foul-smelling gunge. A brief rinse at a town waterpipe was all I could manage before warily presenting myself at the most run-down hotel I could find in the hope that the management would be less discriminating about their clientele. Luckily I found an establishment whose concierge appeared to have no sense of smell.

For once, I settled into my urban surroundings more with relief than nostalgia for the heights I'd left behind. Don't get me wrong, I love my tent, but a hot bath has its place in the world too.

9

A Peripatetic Highpoint

SO YOU WISH to climb the highest summit in the land. That would be Ben Nevis. Everybody knows that. No problem. The highest summit in a foreign land? No problem. You'll find its name and location in a guidebook or on the internet. France? Mont Blanc. Greece? Mount Olympus. Azerbaijan? Mount Bazarduzu. You knew that anyway. Norway? Ah, now we have a problem.

First answer this question: what do you consider to be the 'summit' of a mountain? Obviously, the highest point. But what if we build an observatory or restaurant on top. Is the summit now the highest point of the building? What if we erect a cross or large rock cairn? Does this raise the height of the mountain?

Most of us would probably say that man-made elevations shouldn't count. But what about ice and snow? If three metres of winter snow cap Ben Nevis, is it three metres higher in winter than in summer? Perhaps not... but you'll nevertheless have to climb three metres higher to reach the top.

What if the snow forms a permanent layer, as it does on the higher mountains of the world? Should the icy top of Mount Everest count as the summit? Or should we discount the ice and count the topmost rocky bit beneath it as the summit? If we count snow and ice, as current visual cartographic methods do, then mountains' heights will vary according to climatic change. Which brings us back to Norway.

The highest mountain in Norway lies in the Jotunheimen (Home of the Giants) and is one of two contenders: Galdhøpiggen and Glittertind. The highest point on Galdhøpiggen's rocky summit (excluding summit buildings) is 2,469m. The highest point of solid rock on nearby Glittertind is 2,452m, but this is submerged beneath by an ice cap. For much of the 20th century the ice exceeded 17m in thickness and, as this seemed to be a relatively permanent situation, Glittertind was considered to be the highest mountain.

However, climatic change has caused the ice cap to shrink. At the time of writing, it is only 13m thick. This gives Glittertind a height of 2,465m and forces it to bow to Galdhøpiggen as Norway's highest mountain.

A similar situation may arise in future on Sweden's highest mountain, Kebnekaise. The rocky, ice-free north top is 2,096m. The glaciated south top has traditionally been regarded as the summit with a height of 2,111m, but like Glittertind it has lost ice and hence height in recent years. In time it may become lower than the north top, although this eventuality is by no means certain. In 2012, for instance, the ice layer grew by 2.1m, raising the south top's height to 2,101.8m.

Given climatic uncertainty, and cartographic methods that use visual data to determine elevation, the only foolproof way to climb Norway's highest mountain is to climb both Glittertind *and* Galdhøpiggen. Fortunately for hillwalkers, this is easy because both are no more than walk-ups from Visdalen, the deep valley that separates them.

At the head of the Visdalen road stands Spiterstulen Lodge, a time-honoured base that has catered to hillwalkers since 1836. The present main building, built in 1934, is a grand affair containing a cafeteria, a dance floor, a swimming pool, a terrace with a crackling log fire and beautiful pine furnishings. Breakfast – the famous Scandinavian *smörgåsbord* – is such a treat that you can buy a postcard of it as a memento.

From this 1,100m base, the rival Norwegian highpoints can be bagged in turn. Of the two mountains, Glittertind is by far the more spectacular peak, rising in splendid isolation, its summit at the very edge of 200m cliffs dropping sheer to the Grotbreen glacier. The glacial environment lends an air of seriousness to the ascent, but the summit ice cap is completely crevasse-free and can be crossed without ice-axe or crampons. In summer, a good trail in soft snow points the way.

My companion Anne and I traversed the mountain from east

Crossing the summit of Glittertind

to west en route to Spiterstulen during a backpacking tour of the Jotunheimen. On ascent from the east, the snow trail triumphantly balanced two conflicting needs. It managed not only to keep safely back from the cliff edge overlooking the Grotbreen glacier but also to stay close enough to it to allow fantastic views of the beetling cornice that overhung the abyss.

The descent of the west side to Spiterstulen, out of sight of the cliffs, was never going to match that for scenic interest. Happily, the mountain gods had seen fit to provide a long, easy snow gully beside the trail, and this gave a romping descent that was pure fun.

To avoid the crowds at Spiterstulen, we camped across the river from the lodge and splashed out only on the unmissable *smörgåsbord* the following morning. Suitably replenished, we set off packless for a return trip to the summit of Galdhøpiggen – a snow-free ascent of around four hours. We climbed out of sun into cloud, buffeted by the bitter wind that was our constant companion in the Jotunheimen. You didn't have to close your eyes to imagine you were on a Scottish winter ascent.

The summit was busy and, much to our surprise, sported a café selling hot drinks and souvenirs. Thankfully, I'd brought some kroner with me so was able to purchase a summit badge and certificate (I'm a sucker for kitsch).

The following day, we bade farewell to Spiterstulen and continued our Jotunheimen trek southwest into much wilder country. In barren moonscapes far from the crowds, we camped beneath fierce rock peaks, where cornices collapsed into remote lakes with a great roar, sending tidal waves bursting over their shores. We climbed some peaks and failed to climb others, but of one thing we were sure – we had *definitely* climbed Norway's highest mountain... whichever it is.

10

Bottoming the Inverted Mountain

AS I STOOD at the bottom of the Grand Canyon, I recalled the warnings against attempting to hike there and back in a single day. Above me stretched a mind-numbing 4,500ft climb back to civilisation in over 110°F (40°C) heat. As the rock shimmered in the heat haze and the steep switchbacks of the Devil's Corkscrew rose before me, I wondered – had I taken on too much?

When first seen from the canyon rim, the 277-miles-long scar in the Arizona desert is too vast to comprehend. Only as the sun crosses the sky does the changing interplay of light and shadow highlight the canyon's three-dimensional, maze-like internal structure.

Gradually, the countless sub-canyons and buttes that together form this gaping hole in the earth's crust begin to take on individuality. It becomes apparent that some of the buttes beneath your feet are 4,000ft mountains rising from the canyon bottom, isolated from each other by deep side canyons. They rise as towering walls of rock that resemble Japanese pagodas or Mayan temples. Their names reflect their exotic appearance: Osiris Temple, Wotan's Throne, Cheops Pyramid, Tower of Ra.

These mountains are rarely climbed. The summit of Shiva Temple, for example, remained untrodden until 1937, when Harold E. Anthony of the American Museum of Natural History led an expedition to scale it. Scientists speculated that the summit, cut off from north and south rims for thousands of years, might harbour dinosaurs or other forms of life that had evolved separately. The press sensationalised the expedition as a climb to the Lost World, but in the event no new species were discovered.

The more I stared at the canyon and its mountains, the more it did indeed look like a lost world, and soon I was itching to go over the edge and explore. The classic hike from Canyon Village, where roads and railway converge on the 7,000ft-high south rim, is rim to river and back. It is usually undertaken as a two-day hike or mule trip, with an overnight stay in the canyon bottom at Bright Angel Campground or Phantom Ranch, where there are bunkhouses and a canteen. Rangers routinely advise against attempting a day trip, but they do it themselves, and the record from north to south rim is held by a Native American girl who took just four hours. How hard could it be?

In an odd reversal of normal hillwalking practice, the day would begin with an early morning descent and end with a long climb back up in the baking heat of the afternoon, with no escape route. I proposed to descend the waterless, seven-mile long South Kaibab Trail and re-ascend the ten-mile long Bright Angel Trail, which is longer but has water at various points.

I went over the edge on the South Kaibab soon after dawn. Leaving the hustle and bustle of the south rim behind, a series of steep switchbacks descended into a magical landscape hidden from above. Across the canyon rose two fantastic peaks – the terraced Brahma Temple and the pagoda-like Zoroaster Temple, whose increasingly Matterhorn-like appearance was to dominate the rest of the descent. Beyond it soared the scarcely less impressive Thor Temple and Wotan's Throne, all these peaks clustered round a great basin known as the Ottoman Amphitheatre. It was as though I was walking not into a canyon but into a mountain wonderland.

Two-thirds of the way down, at minus 3,000ft, the trail levelled out onto a curious shelf known as the Tonto Plateau where, in summer temperatures that can reach 120°F (50°C), cactus and sage brush thrive and animals such as rabbits and rats practise a form of summer hibernation called estivation. It was an adaptation to heat that became increasingly appealing to me as the temperature rose ever higher.

At the far edge of the plateau, the trail plunged into the secret gorge of the inner canyon, and suddenly there it was – the mighty Colorado River, the canyon-maker itself, an irresistible force over 500ft wide. A final set of switchbacks took me down to the Black Bridge, which I crossed to reach the side canyon of Bright Angel Creek.

Hot, dusty and parched, I shuffled along the creekside, past the campground with its lovely shaded picnic tables, to the huts at Phantom Ranch, set among irrigated fields and spreading cottonwood trees. The canteen turned out to be a wonderful, air-conditioned oasis selling snacks and chilled homemade lemonade that was pure nectar. I stoked up on the stuff until my stomach ached, and swapped stories with other hikers, muleteers and river runners.

Such an idyllic spot was difficult to leave. Stepping outside again was like walking into a shimmering wall of heat you could almost touch. I moseyed back to the Colorado, dipped a hand in the swirling, chocolate-coloured current as a symbolic gesture and re-crossed at the Silver Bridge. The open construction of this second of the canyon's two bridges makes it possible to see the surging torrent beneath one's feet – a disconcerting experience. Mules refuse to cross it.

Back on the near side of the river, the short River Trail led to the start of the Bright Angel Trail, which would be my return route to the rim. Strength-sapping riverside sand dunes made tough going in the oven-like conditions, and that was even

In the heart of the Grand Canyon on the South Kaibab

before the ascent began. Above towered cliff upon cliff, mountain upon mountain. It was difficult to believe that civilisation lay up there somewhere.

The Bright Angel Trail began its ascent with deceptive gentleness but soon gave a taste of what was to come at the steep switchbacks of the Devil's Corkscrew. They say that on ascent you lose two pints of liquid per hour, so I tackled the Corkscrew slowly, trying to maintain a murmur of air around my body. Lizards scampered nonchalantly across my path, as though they knew I would not have the energy to disturb them.

Above the switchbacks lay Garden Creek and, like so many others who passed this way, I plunged into its cool, refreshing waters. Again, it was a difficult spot to leave, but at least it wasn't far now to Indian Gardens, back on the Tonto Plateau, where Garden Creek Springs erupted from the rock to irrigate the parched land.

The gardens are a true oasis in the desert and were once farmed by Havasupai Indians, who still live in the canyon further downriver. Today there are toilets, a ranger station and a campground. Fountains provide drinking water. Beautiful cottonwood trees planted in the 1900s provide shade for benches and picnic tables.

I sat heat-dazed beneath the trees, mesmerised by the sound of leaves rustling in the breeze. Tourists who had come down from the rim for the day looked fitter and more bright-eyed, but many had overstretched themselves and would struggle to make it back up the 3,000ft climb.

Above Garden Springs, the south rim cliffs rose in an almost unbroken sweep, uncluttered by side canyons, ridges and buttes. The trail climbed gradually towards the cliff foot and entered merciful late afternoon shadow. Resthouses at three miles and one and a half miles below the rim would provide further water, so all that was required now to complete the ascent was determination.

The trail tackled the cliffs in a series of seemingly interminable switchbacks, beginning with an especially steep section known as Jacob's Ladder. The miles were long but time passed slowly as lengthening shadows delineated previously unnoticed rock features below.

When succeeding bursts of determination seemed to bring me no nearer the top, it became increasingly harder to keep placing one foot in front of the other. Grand Canyon topography distorts perceptions, making the rim seem ever closer but indefinitely unreachable, so few who climb from the bottom are not staggering a little as they near the top. As encouragement, whoops of joy from those who had reached the rim drifted down from above, while the surreal whistle of a steam train echoed around the canyon walls.

It came as a surprise to find that there was suddenly no more trail. One second I was struggling ever upwards, the next I had left the vertical for the horizontal and emerged onto the south rim into a different world of hotels, shops, restaurants and crowds. I took one last, wistful glance over my shoulder at the yawning depths below, passed a fat chipmunk who looked at me with a patronising air, and headed for the nearest Häagen-Dazs.

11

The Big One In One Day

THEY CALL IT The Big One, and in the lower 48 states they don't come any bigger. 14,505ft (4,121m) of towering rock (according to the latest surveys). Mount Whitney – the highest mountain in the USA outside Alaska.

Eleven thousand feet below the summit, in the one-horse town of Lone Pine, it was 5.30am. At Bobo's Bonanza, truckers tucked into gargantuan breakfasts while I toyed sleepily with a plate of over-easy eggs and hash browns. They only had to climb back into their cabs. I was contemplating a single-day return to the summit of The Big One.

I'd managed to bottom the Grand Canyon in a day, but this would require a whole new order of effort. From the road end at Whitney Portal above Lone Pine, at a height of 8,360ft, the return trip to the summit would involve a hike of 22 miles and over 6,000ft of ascent, much of it at high altitude.

Most prospective summiteers overnight at Trail Camp, half-way up at 12,040ft, but this requires a wilderness permit and all are snapped up months in advance. The only option for a foreign or passing hiker is to obtain a day permit. Even these are hard to come by at the height of summer, but I was lucky enough to find that July snow on the trail had reduced demand. As an additional incentive for a single-day ascent, local stores peddled a t-shirt bearing a sketch of the peak and the legend The Big One In One Day. I wanted that t-shirt, but first I had to earn it.

Whitney is located in the Sierra Nevada of California, whose eastern front towers 10,000ft (3,000m) and more over the Owens Valley to form one of the great mountain escarpments of the world. Most of the high peaks are hidden away in the interior, but Whitney rears up in full frontal abandon, proudly showing all it has to offer. From Lone Pine in the valley, its skyline forms a frieze of jagged needles, making it so difficult to pick out the true summit that early explorers even climbed the wrong one by mistake.

As I drove up to Whitney Portal, pre-dawn light etched the eastern wall of the Sierra a ghostly white, flattening all detail and making any easy ascent from this side seem impossible. Only when the sun broke above the rim of the Inyo mountains on the far side of the Owens Valley did the rock turn from white to a more inviting pink and then red. Whitney's abrupt summit buttress beckoned like a finger. It was the last I was to see of it for some time.

Whitney Portal lies at the foot of a craggy, forested, claustrophobic basin low down on the mountain, and the trail first has to work its convoluted way up out of that basin. In easy-angled switchbacks in the early morning shade of pinyon pines, it climbed steadily past Lone Pine Lake and Mirror Lake to emerge at the lovely meadow known as Trail Camp. It was not until here, a whole 3,680ft above the Portal, that the huge rock wall that forms the east face of Whitney and its satellites burst into view with spectacular suddenness.

From Mount Muir at one end to Mount Whitney at the other, a succession of jagged peaks stabbed the impossibly blue sky – Third Needle, Day Needle, Keeler Needle – classic rock peaks famed in the history of American big wall climbing. It was a jaw-dropping reward for having come this far, but at the same time it was obvious that the whole climb up to this point had been mere foreplay for what lay ahead.

Trail Camp, with the last sure water en route, is the main base for the ascent of Whitney, and it was busy. Tents added colour to the now burning rockscape and prospective summiteers stood around contemplating and looking skyward. There were still nearly 2,500ft to go.

Apart from its magnificent setting, the main attraction of Trail Camp for hikers used to be its solar-powered toilet. However, this proved to be too popular. After one season alone, six tons of waste had to be airlifted out. (Old Trail Camp joke: How do

The two-lane blacktop to Mount Whitney (centre left)

they advertise the position of pilot? – Person wanted to take the crap out of Whitney). The toilet was removed in 2004 and all hikers (day or overnight) are now required to carry a WAG bag (a 'toilet in a bag') and bring down their own waste. Another makeshift toilet at Whitney summit was removed in 2007, so there are now none on the mountain.

Beyond Trail Camp, in full view now of the peaks above, it felt as though the real ascent was just beginning. Leaving greenery behind for a starker world of granite, 96 switchbacks climbed a steep slope of rocks and scree that rose 1,700ft to Trail Crest at 13,777ft. For the sake of sanity, I decided not to count them, but this proved as difficult as forcing oneself not to think of something. At one point, chain handrails aided progress through late-lying winter snow on an exposed section that would otherwise have been too dangerous to pass.

Trail Crest, as its name implied, marked the spot where the trail reached the skyline. It's a popular rest spot, not just for some much needed R&R but also to take in the suddenly revealed western view over the Sierra Nevada, with mountain upon mountain receding to the horizon.

Only 2.5 miles and 720ft of ascent to go now, but altitude was to make it the toughest part of the route. The trail turned northwards, rising across gentle slopes on the far side of the sharp crest that connects Mount Muir and the needles to Mount Whitney. The 'windows' between the needles opened up vertiginous views of the shimmering Owens Valley far below.

My breath came in gasps and movement became painfully slow. Curiously, time seemed to slow down along with me, as though I was in a slow-motion movie. Every moment was stretched to such an extent that, despite the exertion, there was time to examine and savour it. I have never experienced such heightened awareness on a mountain, before or since.

Seven hours after I'd set out, the gradient eased beneath my feet and I found myself on the great flat plateau summit that is the roof of America. I collapsed to the ground, scarcely able to believe I'd made it. All around the compass, mountains pierced the sky as far as the eye could see, but not one single point was higher. It was a poignant moment.

There were about a dozen of us at the summit and pretty soon we were all buddies. We took photographs of each other grinning inanely. Food and tales were swapped. We needed to share our elation. I lay on my stomach on the cliff-top and peered over the edge of the abyss, Below me, a helmeted figure defied gravity as he progressed slowly up the East Face, a Class 4 climb that in 1939 became the first big wall route on the west coast.

One by one my summit companions left. I would never have the place to myself because some intended to bivouac and see in the dawn, but that was okay. We were fellow souls. Finally it was time for me to leave also, with one last longing look and a promise. There were 11 long miles to go to Whitney Portal, but it was all downhill, the prospect of nightfall added further incentive for a swift descent and above all, there was a t-shirt to buy.

12

In the Wake of the Gold Rush

IN THE DARKNESS we converge on the small hut in the clearing in the woods. There must be about 50 of us. The river roars beside our tents. A low ceiling of black cloud rumbles overhead. Rain slants down in the beams from our head torches. We assemble inside the hut, pressed close together, our bodies steaming. A hush descends over the gathering and Mike takes centre stage. Mike is the resident ranger and he gives this talk every night. We listen attentively as he doles out advice, patiently answering the questions on everyone's lips and raising anticipation.

What's it like at the top? Pretty awesome, but we'll probably not see much as there's a 70 per cent chance of rain. What's the trail like? Pretty rough. Will there be snow? Some. Will we make it? Most people do – start early and just take it easy. Reluctant to leave this motivational gathering, we retire to our tents and lie in our sleeping bags listening to the sound of heavy raindrops on canvas, each alone with our thoughts.

I was attempting perhaps the most famous hiking trail in the world: the Chilkoot Trail, which has been called 'the most beautiful 33 miles in Alaska and British Columbia', 'the meanest 33 miles in history' and 'the world's longest museum'.

What makes the route unique is its fascinating combination of spectacular scenery and stirring history. It is one of only three glacier-free routes from the Pacific coast to the Canadian interior and was the route used by hordes of prospectors ('sourdoughs') to reach the newly discovered gold fields of the Yukon. The hardships that the sourdoughs endured during the Klondike Gold Rush have become the stuff of legend, immortalised in early photographs and first-person accounts. The trail is still littered with their artefacts, which it is a criminal offence to remove.

The route begins at Dyea, an old Gold Rush ghost town just

outside Skagway. Reaching the picturesque little town of Skagway is an adventure in itself, requiring an ambitious 1,538-mile drive up the ALCAN Highway from Vancouver or an expensive multi-day cruise up the Pacific coast. The trail climbs the valley of the Taiya River all the way to Chilkoot Pass, a notch in the Coast Range on the Alaskan–Canadian border, 16.5 miles from and 1,140m above the sea-level start. On the far side of the pass the trail descends past several lakes to Lake Bennet, set in roadless wilderness a further 16.5 miles away. From here sourdoughs continued their journey to the gold fields by boat. The way back to Skagway for modern-day hikers is by train, about which more later.

The trail takes four to five days to complete and is pretty rugged in places, but its tough reputation stems more from sourdough tales than from technical difficulty. In summer, there is nothing here to trouble any backpacker of reasonable fitness and experience. The main negative factor is the weather on the near (American) side of the pass, which is nearly always wet. Surprisingly, this is less depressing than might be imagined. Once on the trail, surrounded by historical memorabilia, you soon enter Chilkoot Mode, a peculiar condition in which the more the wind and rain whips around, the more you feel you are tackling the trail as it was meant to be tackled, as the sourdoughs tackled it. And you can expect to walk into sunshine on the Canadian side of the pass.

At one time Dyea was home to no less than 10,000 prospectors. Hard to imagine now. No buildings remain and the only relic of the old days is Slide Cemetery, the resting place of some of the 70 victims of the terrible avalanche that took place along the trail near Sheep Camp on 3 April 1898. As if to prepare the unconditioned hiker for tough times ahead, the trail begins with a steep ascent and descent around riverside crags before it levels off through woods to follow the Taiya River to Finnegan's Point at Mile 4.9. Here my partner Wendy and I pitched camp.

The following morning we awoke to drizzle and trekked on beneath dripping trees, with cloud swirling through the canopy overhead. The warm air was too much for our so-called breathable waterproofs to handle. Steep sections of trail soon had them clogged with sweat, leaving us damp and uncomfortable.

At 7.8 miles we reached Canyon City, former residence of 1,500 souls. A footbridge gave access to the remains of the 'city' on the far bank, where there was an old cooker, a steam boiler and various rusted iron contraptions whose function I couldn't even begin to guess at. Everything else had been reclaimed by the forest.

The next section of trail had changed little since a prospector described it as 'the worst piece of trail on the route'. It stayed high above the canyon through the dense, dripping forest, continually climbing up and down, beset by boulders and tree roots. At one point the mists parted sufficiently for a view of the river far below. In that terrible winter of 1878–9, the sourdoughs had climbed the frozen river itself, surmounting icefalls on rickety ladders.

A riverside clearing above the head of the canyon at Mile 10 announced our arrival at Pleasant Camp, whose name reflects what a wonderful sight it must have been to the sourdoughs. As so often on the trail, we were astounded to learn that there used to be a restaurant here. Nothing now.

Beyond Pleasant Camp the trail improved and we made good time to Sheep Camp at Mile 13, the traditional second night campsite and summer residence of Mike the Ranger. At the height of the Gold Rush this base camp for the Chilkoot Pass was home to 8,000 people, 14 restaurants, three saloons, two dance halls and countless other buildings. Impossible to imagine now, but it was known as the City of Tents.

In historic diaries at the hut, I discovered we weren't the first visitors from Scotland. One morning in 1898, a trumpet blast rent the air: 'Then a voice – "Is that you, Scottie?" "Aye, it's me, and I'll gie ye Auld Lang Syne frae the summit the morn."'

We could have done with Scottie the next morn, as we slept through our 7am alarm and awoke at 8.30am to find our fellow trekkers already gone. The trail continued to climb steadily in the rain until the dripping trees thinned out, only to be replaced by luxuriant, soaking trailside vegetation that brushed wetly against our legs. Thank goodness for Chilkoot Mode.

At Mile 16 we reached The Scales – the site where the sourdoughs had to prove to the Canadian Mounties that they had enough equipment and supplies to continue. Here the past came vividly alive with the remains of an old gun holster, smashed plates from a former restaurant, lots of unfathomable ironmongery and woodwork and, above all, some soles of boots, still nailed around the edges. And in the bog nearby: a complete shoe, made from a rigid sole with a canvas upper. Just lying there in the bog. What had happened to its owner?

The summit of the Pass was now only half a mile away, but that half mile was the most notorious part of the trail – a steep gully of large boulders known as the Golden Staircase. If there is a single image that captures the spirit of the Gold Rush, it is that taken in the winter of 1897–8 of an unbroken procession of sourdoughs climbing the Golden Staircase, deep in snow, bent double beneath the weight of their loads, striving ever upwards to the summit of the pass. It has become a metaphor for the indomitability of the human spirit.

We scrambled up the Golden Staircase through thick mist and over boulders and patches of snow. Finally, at Mile 16.5, we arrived at the American summit hut. Nearby was another hut where Dan, the Canadian ranger, lived during the summer season. He was playing host to his American counterpart Mike when we arrived, but he still had time to strike a winning blow for Canadian hospitality by offering us mugs of hot lemonade.

Having crossed the international border, we began the easier descent of the north side of the pass. The trail dropped below the cloud and at Mile 17.5 reached craggy Crater Lake, whose shoreline sands gave eerie walking as the mist parted and swirled. With clearing sky at last, we began to appreciate the immensity of the land and the ambition of the sourdoughs. Written on the wall of the summit hut was a letter one of them had written in 1897: '… before us vastness, silence, grandeur…

Into Canada

In order to feel your own smallness and insignificance, stand on the summit... and realise what an atom in this great universe you are.'

The miles came more easily now, with expansive lake scenery that more than compensated for the wooded vistas of the American side. Passing the end of Morrow Lake, the trail descended a gorge to Happy Camp at Mile 21.5 then continued high above Long Lake to a wonderfully scenic camp on the shores of Deep Lake. Here we pitched the tent and aired damp gear, investigated yet more old Gold Rush artefacts and sat in the sun eating wild berries.

The following morning we reluctantly struck camp and set off for our last day on the trail. The route led around the shores of Deep Lake and descended Deep Lake Canyon, where it became a fast, smooth trail down to Lindeman City on Lake Lindeman at Mile 25.5. In Gold Rush days, Lindeman City and Lake Bennet beyond were jumping off points for the next stage of the journey to the gold fields – a perilous 550-mile boat journey along the Yukon River.

We visited the lonely hilltop cemetery, whose site is given added poignancy by a display of some lines from Robert Service's evocative poem 'The Law of the Yukon': 'This is the Law of the Yukon, that only the Strong shall thrive; That surely the Weak shall perish, and only the Fit survive.' We checked out Gold Rush mementoes in the exhibit tent and purchased a trail certificate of which I was inordinately proud.

Onwards we trekked, the trail undulating across hilly terrain beside six-miles-long Lake Lindeman. At Loon Lake I sat in the woods, happy as a bear, scooping handfuls of luscious huckleberries from the bushes around me while the sun beat down in short polar slants. The final mile to Lake Bennet crossed sandy ground through trees and seemed to take forever, but finally there it was – Lake Bennet, the end of the trail.

There are no roads here, but a restored narrow gauge railway provides a lifeline back to the trail's starting point. We joined other backpackers on the platform, downed our packs and waited for the train. Soon we were relaxing in style in an old Wild West carriage as the train carried us effortlessly out of the wilderness and back to the fleshpots of Skagway.

After four hard days on the trail, the return to civilisation felt too swift. I sat at a pleasant boardwalk café, happily sipping a reviving cappuccino, but my heart was still in the wilds.

13

Excelsior among the Bark Eaters

POSTHOLING INTO Avalanche Lake is not an eventuality that bears thinking about, but the ice looks thick, the 'hitch up Matildas' seem superfluous and Wendy and I snowshoe out across the surface of the lake like true Bark Eaters. This is the most spectacular hike in the Adirondacks and we aren't going to turn back now. The wind is head-on and stings our faces with swirling spindrift. Down at Marcy Dam ranger station, the thermometer registered minus 12°C. We can only guess at the wind chill now. To my layers of thermal vest, shirt, fleece and anorak I add a down waistcoat.

The lake is spectacular – an eye-shaped expanse of ice squeezed between walls of rock that in places rise vertically from the shore. In summer, progress along the shoreline is possible only by following a contorted trail that in places has to resort to wooden catwalks over the water. These catwalks are known as 'hitch up Matildas' after a Victorian lady who came here in pre-catwalk days. Too modest to wrap her thighs around the neck of the guide who was attempting to carry her, Matilda slid down his back and was encouraged to 'hitch up' before she dipped her nether regions into the water.

In winter, frozen rivers and lakes have always provided the easiest corridors for foot travel in the Adirondacks of northern New York State, and Avalanche Lake is no exception. In fact, it is more easily negotiated in winter than in summer. The frozen surface is carpeted with snow and we shuffle across the powdery surface in our snowshoes. Overhead, cottonwool clouds tumble across the sky, with the sun shining brightly in between to cast ever-changing patterns of light and shade on the snow.

In the middle of the lake, we stop to admire the furrow of snow that marks our progression from the shore. Above us, great rock walls rise in tiers on either side to Mount Colden and Algonquin Peak, at 1,559m the second highest mountain in the Adirondacks and our objective for the day. It's a fabulous spot. The walls are known locally as *slides*, after the way in which they were formed, by rock avalanches. It is these avalanches that also formed the lake and gave it its name. The last major avalanche was in 1942, when rockfall raised the water level by three metres.

Snowshoeing through the frozen silence is an exhilarating experience. Winter ascents without cross-country skis or snowshoes are generally impracticable and are in any case disallowed

Crossing Avalanche Lake

on trails that cross land owned by the Adirondack Mountain Club (ADK), which most do. The rule is in force to stop hikers ruining the trails with deep bootholes, or *postholes* as they are called.

Use of cross-country skis on the narrow forest trails is an acquired skill, but snowshoes are easy and addictively entertaining to use. We hire them at Adirondack Loj at the start of the trail, strap them on and simply pad out into the pristine halls of the forest like born Bark Eaters. 'Bark Eaters' is a traditional translation of the word 'Adirondacks', which Mohawks disparagingly applied to a defeated rival tribe and which locals now call themselves with pride.

We tunnel through vast vaults of whiteness, where the snow lies so thickly on the trees that at times the route before us seems to close down. The trail is of ceaseless interest. There are inclined walkways to climb, fallen trees to clamber over and under, thinly iced streams to jump and icy steepenings to negotiate. We learn technique as we go. On steep ground, I find it is possible to kick steps by flicking the back of the snowshoe up and kicking the metal toe horizontally into the snow, but when I try to walk backwards I end up in a heap.

As we approach timberline the trail steepens sharply and the steel claws on the base of our snowshoes scrabble at the icy surface. Then suddenly we emerge into open air above the tree canopy, with the trail now marked by yellow paint marks on bare rock and sheet ice everywhere. We change into crampons, knuckle down into the bitter wind and crunch our way to the summit.

Although we wear neoprene nose masks, facing into the icy blast is almost impossible to bear. Wendy sits down with her back to it while I force myself to take a few snaps and gaze wistfully across Avalanche Lake to the summit dome of Mount Marcy, at 1,629m the highest Adirondack. Next time. Despite the intense cold, I am loath to leave, but a storm is brewing. The Adirondacks are subject to some of the most savage weather in the world, and above treeline is no place to be when it strikes.

The black storm front approaches relentlessly, seeming to gather pace the closer it gets. It hits suddenly, with such brutal ferocity that it becomes difficult to stand upright or see through snow flurries. Hastily, we make a dash for timberline, where the shelter of the trees enables us to marvel in safety at the raging skies above.

After changing back from crampons to snowshoes, we shuffle and slide joyfully back down the trail to the Loj, reluctant for the day to end. Local experts sit on the tail-end of their snowshoes, which raises the front claw free of the snow, and slide down without constraint... or brakes. We weren't tempted.

There's a Latin word that New York State has adopted as its motto: *Excelsior*. After climbing Algonquin Peak, I resolved that, if I am ever granted a coat of arms, it will be my motto too. It means 'Ever Upwards'.

14

3,000m high in the Indian Ocean

IN THE GREAT empty expanse of water that is the Indian Ocean, to the west of South Africa and Madagascar, an undersea volcanic chain breaks water twice to form the charismatic islands of Mauritius and Réunion. Ex-British Mauritius has a mountainous southern half peppered with singular peaks, of which the highest is the Piton de la Petite Rivière Noire (828m). Still-French Réunion is wilder and higher, with the active volcano of the Piton de la Fournaise (2,632m) and a mountainous core that soars to a height of 3,069m at the Piton des Neiges. To the west of the Piton there is no higher mountain at this latitude, close to the Tropic of Cancer, until you have travelled most of the way around the globe, past Australia, and reached the Chilean Andes.

The Mauritian mountains are distinctive and alluring, but hardly anyone climbs them. It's nearly impossible to find a local who even knows where to start. The island is encircled by a coral reef that produces lots of white sand strands and, hard though it is to believe, impoverished souls seem to prefer lying comatose on these.

It's different on Réunion. There are no beaches here and the rugged, mist-enshrined interior is as strange and exotic a botanical garden as any CGI-enhanced fantasy film could envisage. The climate is tropical and the 3,000m elevation differential produces an astonishing variety of flora. At lush lower elevations, mimosa, hibiscus, bougainvillea, jacaranda and others produce a kaleidoscope of colour. Fields of sugar cane, lentils and geraniums (cultivated for their oil) are commonplace. Exotic trees and alpine plants reach towards the heights.

I'd dreamed of going there since, as a teenager, I'd read an

Alan Williams' Réunion-set thriller. I was enthralled by his descriptions of daring roads that wound up exposed mountainsides to remote villages, which themselves were dwarfed by the high peaks above.

The cost and logistics of seeing it all for myself seemed insuperable until, in 1996, there arose an opportunity to lecture at the University of Mauritius (which is another story). Réunion lay only a short, bumpy plane ride away on a rickety old turbo prop. August was not the best time to go (October to March is the dry summer season), but the timing was not mine to choose.

The main draw on Réunion is the trio of high cirques that scallop the Piton des Neiges: Cilaos, Mafate and Salazie. These are no ordinary European-type cirques of the kind found, say, in the Alps. Each is huge and complex, having an area of between 30 and 40 square miles and its own network of trails. The 37-miles-long R1 long-distance trail links the three cirques by climbing over the ridges that separate them and, in so doing, circumnavigating the Piton at a high level. From the trail's 2,478m highpoint, it seemed from the map that the summit itself could be reached, and it was to this end that I had lugged backpacking gear around Mauritius.

The expedition turned into the most incredible and most strenuous of any I have attempted. Cloud forests of vertical mud had me vowing never again to complain about the state of British paths, while the searing heat and humidity made me realise for the first time how lucky British hillwalkers are to live in a temperate climate. But what an adventure!

The route began in the dramatic Cirque de Cilaos, reached by a convoluted road whose negotiation was a thrill ride in itself. Surrounded by high mountain walls (*remparts*) and chock full of canyons, waterfalls and rocky enclaves, it seemed a fantastical place to a humble British hillwalker. Its name is said to derive from a Malagasy word meaning 'the place one never leaves', but the R1 beckoned and its call was irresistible. In steep switchbacks, it climbed 700m up a wooded slope to the 2,082m Col du Taibit then descended more gently for 450m to Marla, a small hamlet in the adjacent Cirque de Mafate. Unused as I was to the exercise, this was quite enough for a first day on the trail.

Mafate was a less dramatic but even more remote spot than Cilaos. Helicopters served the small population that lived there, but otherwise it could only be reached on foot. I camped in a lentil field near a treasure trove of a small grocery store whose ice-cold bière went down a treat.

The following morning broke crisp and clear, as was to be the case every day. Only later, as the rising sun heated the air, did mist rise and envelop the summits. I spent the day packless, exploring the cirque's ravines and waterfalls. At a spectacular spot called Les Trois Roches (The Three Rocks), the river plunged into a narrow slot chasm hidden in the middle of a smooth rock tableland. No wonder canyoneering was such a popular sport on the island.

On Day three, I shouldered my pack once more, climbed out of Mafate and crossed the 1,942m Col de Fourche to the Cirque de Salazie. The 300m ascent was less than half as much as that out of Cilaos but proved an order of magnitude more difficult. After crossing the Plaine des Tamarins, with its strange tamarind trees and their peculiar dangling fruit pods, the route developed into a testing climb through misty woods dripping with moisture. Long stretches of sodden moss had been made passable only by floating rafts of unstable logs across them.

The 1,000m descent of the far side of the col required even more concentration. The steep, slippery trail skirted abrupt dropoffs whose mist-enshrouded depths I was more than content to imagine rather than see, yet the hushed atmosphere in the cloud forest was otherworldly. The silence was broken only by the occasional day-hiker who would loom out of the murk with encouragements of 'Bon Courage!'

The waterfall-studded Cirque de Salazie was the largest and perhaps the most serenely beautiful of the three great cirques. With access by road from the other side of the island, there was a proper village here, called Hell-bourg. It even boasted a patisserie whose delicacies it would have been churlish not to sample.

When I pitched my tent on the village outskirts, all was right with the world, but if I thought the going had been tough so far…

On Day four, I climbed up into the cloud forest once more. The main trail took such a roundabout route that I opted for a more direct variation that knocked a whole four miles off the distance. Mistake.

The abomination of a path was little more than a roller-coaster of ankle-deep mud that climbed through a labyrinth of moisture-laden trees, up and down slippery inclines of wet rock and tangled roots. With a heavy pack, in the heat and humidity, the effort required to straddle the deepest mud and duck under low-lying branches was draining. There were vertical sections of oozing morass that required you to haul yourself up from tree root to tree root. A couple of particularly ridiculous sections would have been impassable without the provision of fixed ladders.

I confess there was much cursing before I rejoined the main trail, a strength-sapping 1,250m above Hell-bourg. Only then did the going ease as the vegetation thinned and bare lava appeared underfoot. A further 300m ascent brought me to a small hut (the Gîte de la Caverne Dufour) at 2,478m, just below the ridge crest that separated Salazie from Cilaos. I pitched my tent. It was from here that I intended to climb the Piton.

There were a few people sardined into the hut and I was able to obtain some much needed water from the precious supply held in a roof tank fed by rain and cloud. As darkness fell, the temperature dropped alarmingly, yet still I was lured outside the tent into the cold night air by an unexpected spectacle: the cloud had dispersed to reveal a sparkling skyscape of strange southern hemisphere stars. The name Piton des Neiges (Snow Peak) had seemed somewhat fanciful, but it was now clear from the low temperature that it could sport an occasional dusting of snow, and that such an occurrence must indeed be worthy of note in the middle of the Indian Ocean.

I shivered all night in my thin summer sleeping bag and refused to leave it the following morning until the sun hit the tent. I emerged blinking into blue-sky sunshine above a sea of

Morning, 3,069m, Indian Ocean

puffy white cloud, with the Piton's summit just visible 600m above. I set off for it in bitter wind, so dazed from the previous day's exertions that I forgot my balaclava and lost precious time returning for it.

Patches of ice glazed the rock. White paint marks indicated the route. Cloud billowed up from below, engulfed me for a moment then fell back as I climbed above it again. It was a race to the summit. The final stretch led up a rocky couloir to the summit ridge and an astonishing aerial view of Cilaos, seen through deep holes in the cloud.

Then the rounded summit itself, an unremarkable spot made exceptional by its breathtaking situation. I was standing on top of the highest point in the Indian Ocean, a whole 3,000m of vertical distance below. The cloud layer stretched in all directions, like a cotton wool cushion on which it seemed possible to float, and beyond that, in every direction, the endless blue sea.

As the cloud crept up the mountainside and my sunlit summit perch dwindled, I seemed to be balancing on a speck of land suspended in the air. It was at the same time both magical and unnerving. Then the cold clammy hand of the cloud grabbed me for good and it was time to leave this spot of which I had so long dreamed and to which I would probably never return.

The remainder of the day passed in a blur. I raced down to the gîte, retrieved tent and pack and descended into the cloud forest one last time. The steep trail down to Cilaos seemed endless. When I finally rolled into the campground, I could barely pitch the tent before falling asleep. But the following morning, as is the way of things, I was already missing the heights.

Twenty years later, the RI is much improved. There are easier variations than the route I followed. In the summer season, the ground is drier. And yet... call me incorrigible, but I'm glad I was afforded the opportunity to hike the RI when it was at its wildest. It's a cliché that the more you put into something, the more you get out of it, but clichés are clichés for a reason. Let those who wish to do so lie in soporific torpor on a Mauritian beach until their skins turn to leather. The memory of that battle in the cloud-swept highlands of Réunion still makes my heart soar as I write.

Eccentric Escapades

15

Coasteering on Skye

WE NO LONGER categorise Britain as a seafaring nation, but in former times the sea was often the primary means not just of trading and warmongering, but also of transport and communication. This was especially true of remote areas whose topography impeded the building of roads, and nowhere is this more apparent than on Skye, whose coastline is the most complex in the country.

On the map the island resembles a group of five peninsulas joined together in the middle: Sleat, Waternish, Trotternish, Minginish and Duirinish. As the eagle flies it is approximately 50ml long by 7–25ml wide, yet the coastline is so contorted that it's around 400ml long.

And what a coastline it is. With a vertical range that runs from zero (less than zero at low tide) to over 300 metres, there are still few stretches that carry a road. As a result, it remains virtually unknown and untrodden, but this wasn't always the case. Until a couple of centuries ago, travellers and invaders arrived from all points of the compass, not just by the short crossing from Kyle to Kyleakin, where the Skye bridge now stands.

The treacherous Black Skerry off Duirinish claimed many a passing boat and attracted unscrupulous types in search of plunder. The wrecker and smuggler Campbell of Ensor even lit false beacons here to lure ships to their doom.

Huge sea stacks abound. The tallest of the trio, known as MacLeod's Maidens, is 63m high and requires a 4.5ml each-way walk to reach. Stac an Tuill (Hole Stack) resembles a gothic cathedral, complete with spire and vaulted window (the hole). The Stacan Gobhlach (Forked Stacks) are linked to the shore by a double line of great flat rocks, like a giant's stepping stones. None of these are easy to view from the land.

Forgotten sea caves have a long history of occupation. In Waternish, Macrimmon pipers were packed off to caves to practise out of earshot. The Pipers' Cave at Harlosh Point, the largest sea cave on Skye, was once so famous that it was visited by Samuel Johnson and James Boswell on their celebrated 1773 tour of Scotland. Spar Cave in Sleat is one of the natural wonders of Scotland, even if its stalactites have long since been removed for souvenirs.

Lady Grange's Cave is named for a tragic woman who had the misfortune to overhear a Jacobite plot in Edinburgh in 1730. For this, she was abducted and made to eke out the remainder of her life in sometimes appalling conditions on various Hebridean islands, including in this Duirinish cave, until her death in 1745.

Some stretches of coastline are still not fully explored. As recently as 2006, the newly discovered Uamh an Eich Bhric (Cave of the Speckled Horse) yielded a number of important archaeological finds, including the top of a human skull.

One of my favourite coastal formations, accessible only at low tide, is a huge archway cave at the headland of Meall Greepa (Precipice Hill). It tunnels right through the headland to form a beautifully arched cavern some 40m long by 10m high. I know of no one who even knows it's there, never mind visits it.

For years, I was equally ignorant, until a week of cloud on the Cuillin had me looking coastward for exercise. It was a revelation. There was a whole new world of adventure here. How could a single island be so blessed, to have not only the Cuillin, but now also, it seemed, a coast that was equally spectacular?

My desire to discover this secret coast soon led me to realise that it could be every bit as demanding as the mountains. Much of it is as distant from the nearest road as are the summits of the Cuillin. Cliffs often overhang, undercut by the sea. Their vertiginous edges are often crumbling and honeycombed by

Lorgasdal coastal architecture

rabbits. Sheep paths at the cliff edge make for excellent going but can also induce a false sense of security, for sheep have small, cloven feet and no sense of vertigo. Rivers cut deep gorges as they fall to the sea, forming countless unnamed waterfalls that may require appreciable inland detours to outflank. There is rarely any shelter from the elements.

The terrain is often undulating, requiring constant ascent and descent, sometimes on steep, exposed hillsides of grass that become slippery when wet. Such is the height of Skye cliff-tops that total ascent for a route can easily equal that for a hill walk. A different mental attitude from hillwalking is required as the end point of the walk is hardly ever in view.

Even shoreline walking on Skye can be difficult. There are no long sandy strands here, as in the Outer Hebrides. Rocks can be greasy and slippery. Crags can be awkward or even impossible to negotiate. Stonefall, sometimes induced by seabirds, is a danger at the foot of cliffs. Nesting birds can be aggressive and swoop to attack. And the greatest danger of all: becoming trapped at the cliff-foot by an incoming tide.

Over the years, I have come to know the Skye coast intimately and have had as much adventure here as on the Cuillin. Beneath a mile of sea-cliffs on the east coast of Trotternish, I raced an incoming tide to reach safety on return from the Eaglais Bhreugach (False Church) – an enormous boulder split by a huge arch, which is said to have been a site of pagan rites. On the shores of Loch Bracadale, beneath another line of sea-cliffs, I was attacked by nesting terns, whose outstretched talons came so close that I again had to run for safety.

On the north coast, to stay upright, I leant at 45 degrees into an Atlantic gale as I battled to reach the haven of the old coast-guard lookout station, now a small bothy with incredible seaward views. At the top of Biod an Athair, the highest Skye sea cliff at 313m and well named Sky Cliff (*sic* Sky, not Skye), I lay down on the grass at the cliff-edge and peered over the edge at the miniature Atlantic breakers far below.

Miles from any road, between Idrigill Point and Lorgill Bay in Duirinish, there's a remarkable spot. A narrow arête, topped by two pinnacles, drops to the sea. Beside it is a green so perfect that it could surely host a game of bowls. The arête is holed at sea level, forming a natural arch. Beside the arch are two stacks, one a wedge with a knife-edge summit ridge. Between the stacks, the Lorgasdal River plunges into the sea. The scene is the epitome of all that is best in coastal architecture.

For those of us who hanker after more than a coach trip and a tea room, the Cuillin will rightly always be the main attraction on Skye, but the coast deserves to be better known, as it was before that knowledge faded from the collective memory. At least that means there are still some secret and amazing wild places out there, in our united and crowded kingdom, that are just waiting for us to rediscover them.

16

Nutty Deals a Face Plant

IF YOU KNOW anything about me by now, you'll know I was never going to make a great mountain biker. You'll also understand why that hasn't stopped me trying.

The concept of the mountain bike originated in California in the 1960s. Two decades later, my first machine was still viewed with suspicion in the UK, even by me. Off-road, despite its inherent promise of carefree rides up hill and down dale, it was a real boneshaker whose topographical range severely belied its ambition.

Nutty, as it came to be known, earned its 'mountain bike' status solely by dint of possessing a rugged frame and fat tyres. Unlike most of today's models, it spurned suspension, which was still expensive, experimental and, according to the received wisdom of the time, counter-productive to handling.

At the merest suspicion of damp ground ahead, Nutty would squeal to a halt in terror and catapult me over the handlebars to ingest soil samples from a variety of Highland ecosystems. Uphill, like its owner, it refused to change gear under duress and baulked at any gradient above one per cent. Downhill, we both closed our eyes and waited for the inevitable crash.

A brief mountain biking lexicon will give some insight into the nature of our adventures. *Bogging out* is when the front tyre grinds to a halt in mud. This can propel the body forward off the seat and result in a *crotch-tester*. A *cheese grater* is a fall that grinds off skin against gravel, asphalt, bike parts etc. A *handplant* is a crash where your fall is broken by cheese grating your hands.

An *endo* is an abrupt and unorthodox end-over-end dismount, usually resulting in a *face plant* or, at the very least, a *severe gravity check*. *Crayonning* is peppering the ground with bits of skin. A *rockectomy* is the removal of dirt, gravel and whatever other parts of the environment are embedded in the skin. A *mandibular disharmony* occurs when your jaw and the handle-bars attempt to occupy the same space and time.

Nutty and I nevertheless bonded over a series of tough multi-day off-road bike packs through the Highlands. This was helped by the fact that, reluctantly, I agreed to push it much of the way and even carry it over the worst ground. With Nutty over one shoulder and panniers over the other, to balance weight, it was hardly the kind of enterprise those pioneering Californians must have envisaged for their invention. But then they had probably never envisaged attempting to ride the rocks, heather and bog that constitute a typical Scottish mountainside.

Such was the punishment inflicted on Nutty and myself that on one rattling downhill suicide plunge the seat bolt snapped in two and the saddle sheared off, leaving a jagged metal tube projecting alarmingly upwards towards one of the body's more sensitive areas. Fortunately, I was turfed sideways along with the saddle and received only the usual cuts, bruises and soil samples.

Still a long way from road or rail, I cycled the remaining miles by sitting behind the tube, on the rear rack, and reaching forward to steer with my fingertips. I don't need to tell you that was a nerve-shredding ride... but I was more than happy to reach the roadside with *only* my nerves shredded. It was because of this incident that the bike earned its name The Nutcracker.

On occasion, my fellow masochist Simon was crazy enough to accompany me, and this had its advantages. When cycling through swarms of midges, for example, it was comforting to have someone to curse with, although we would have swallowed fewer had we kept our mouths shut. And on one particularly infested evening, we turned on each other in frustration, only half in jest, as the beasties drove us to a frenzy while we attempted to pitch the tent.

On another occasion, I was grateful to the Fates that conspired to visit a puncture on Simon during a bike pack through the roadless country between Dalwhinnie and Fort William. At Corrour Station, the only respite en route, he had to board the train to Fort William with his bike and, in so doing, was able to

Nutty and the author contemplate the main ascent on Comyn's Road

take all my equipment with him. This left me with a gleeful, pack-free run though the wilderness to rejoin him.

Another time, the laugh was on me. Juddering down a rough single-track beside a swollen stream, I hit a *baby-head* (a rock the size of... you guessed it) and was unceremoniously catapulted into the fast-flowing current. As an expert faller, thanks to many years of practice both on foot and in the saddle, I am conditioned to roll on impact in all circumstances. This time I excelled myself by managing to roll in the air, avoid some looming boulders and land safely on my back in the water with a satisfying splash. Drenched though I was, I was proud of my gymnastic dismount and couldn't understand why Simon was doubled up with laughter.

By such means, sometimes alone, sometimes with Simon, Nutty and I explored the Highlands until our joints creaked. Meanwhile, technology moved on, and there came a point when I could no longer ignore the ease with which more modern machines swept past us, their riders changing gear effortlessly while bouncing imperiously aboard new-fangled suspension frames.

Nutty, I'm sad to say, ended its days in the scrap yard. I trust that, wherever it is now, it approves of the new generation of models it begat. I hope too that it wishes me well on my continuing attempts to bond with my new mountain bike on terrain for which the wheel was never going to be fit for purpose.

17

Into Cairngorms Backcountry

NUTTY CAME INTO my life to help me explore the ancient hill tracks that criss-cross the Cairngorms. The most well-known of these are the Lairig Ghru and the Lairig an Laoigh, the two corridor-like passes that thread their way between the peaks of the High Cairngorms. Both lairigs give classic hikes, but on their rugged central sections a bicycle turned out to be no more than an encumbrance. I should have known as much. Even today, with path improvements yielding good off-road cycling at each end of each lairig, the central sections still require a good push. They were nevertheless a walk in the park compared to what Nutty and I were to tackle next.

South of the High Cairngorms, a great mountain barrier separates central Scotland from the north. To travel from Perth to Aviemore, the A9 takes a roundabout route to the west over 460m-high Drumochter Pass, but a number of little-known historic hill tracks take a more direct route further east. It was these that I itched to investigate.

The country here is wonderfully wild and achingly lonely, with extensive moors that climb to the rarely trodden 902m highpoint of Leathad an Taobhain. With no infrastructure and no road access beyond its periphery, you won't find here the crowds that flock to the national park fleshpots of the Aviemore region. It's the kind of place that can make you feel very small indeed, a mere speck of humanity in the vast, uncaring landscape. The sky, often overcast, seems to hover overhead, close enough to touch. I became so taken with the area that I even wrote a book about it: *Exploring Scottish Hill Tracks*.

Few motorists racing up the A9 realise that, a mere five miles east of Drumochter Pass, and only 30m higher, the Gaick (meaning Cleft) provides a shorter through-route by the shores of remote Loch an Duin. If it wasn't for the fact that the loch's steep-sided slopes are notoriously avalanche-prone, 1720s road builder General Wade might well have chosen this way through the mountains instead of Drumochter.

Today, the forgotten Gaick gives an easy point-to-point walk or cycle, mostly on Land Rover tracks out of sight and sound of the busy A9. The outlet stream from Loch an Duin requires a paddle, but this normally presents little problem. There are occasional proposals to build a bridge here and I was once asked to lend my name to one of these, but I couldn't bring myself to condone such an intrusion into the wilds.

East of the Gaick runs a route of even greater antiquity – Comyn's Road, named for a local earl who is said to have been so partial to the ale at a Blair inn that he built the road to transport it back north to his castle at Ruthven. The road has a long military history, being trodden among others by Edward I during his invasion of Scotland in 1295, and it was also the subject of perhaps Scotland's first right-of-way agreement in 1500. Yet how many Cairngorms visitors of today have even heard of it?

Like the Gaick, Comyn's Road now has Land Rover tracks at each end, but the central section crosses moors where the way is so overgrown that it is more easily picked out by aerial reconnaissance. On two wheels it makes for tough going, especially on the main drag, a 380m climb up which Nutty demanded to be carried. Despite or because of its faded glory, it remains a haunting route that has a wonderful air of spaciousness and the feel of the Middle Ages about it. It deserves to be better known.

Further east again is the Minigaig, which succeeded Comyn's Road as the route of choice in the 17th century. The name's derivation is obscure, but it certainly doesn't mean 'mini' as in 'small'. As a through-route to the north, it's a staggering 15 miles shorter than the A9. Wade dismissed it as an alternative to Drumochter Pass only because its height rendered it snowbound in winter. This was of little consequence to the hardy Highlanders of old, for whom directness was more important than the amount of ascent involved. No one travelled in winter anyway.

Canny cattle drovers continued to use the Minigaig even after Wade built his new road, not only because it was shorter but also because it avoided the toll that had to be paid at Drumochter until 1878. Today, it still carries a surprisingly good path for most of its length. As with Comyn's Road, the central section is unridable, but it continues to provide adventure aplenty for the irredeemably intrepid.

My first attempt to cross the Minigaig was on one of those days when horizontal rain sweeps across the moors, burn crossings become hazardous and a head-on gale makes every pedal push a Sisyphean effort. Nutty and I were ignominiously driven back to the Allt Schiecheachain bothy, where I spent a chilly hour trying to coax a few flickering flames from some damp twigs of heather before retreating to a Blair Atholl hostelry.

We made it across the high moors on our second attempt, and that first battle made it all the more satisfying. Some things in life shouldn't come too easily.

East of the Minigaig, deep glens (Tilt, Geldie, Feshie) combine to make a more obvious low-level through-route, and a road has been proposed here on several occasions. For now, thankfully, the glens remain inviolate. May they always remain so. Further east again, the one road that does cut through the mountain barrier is the A93, but perhaps we should not begrudge one access road to Braemar and the ski slopes of Glen Shee.

From the A9 to the A93, the roadless country stretches for over 30 miles as the eagle flies, and eastwards again lies an equally wide tract of empty country known as the Mounth. Cue another group of ancient hill tracks: Causey Mounth, Cairn-a-Mounth, Firmounth, Capel Mounth, the Monega Road and others. There's even a way known as the Smugglers' Shank, which was used to transport illicit whisky from Deeside to all parts south.

Despite their age, these old Mounth tracks remain in good condition and are still well used, often for approaches to popular Munros such as Lochnagar. Two are so high that they even cross the shoulders of Munros close to the summits: Tolmount and Mount Keen. The very names rekindle such memories that, even as I write, I ache again for that high, lonely land. Time to break out the map and plot another expedition...

18

Above the Great Salt Lake

IN THE MIDDLE of northern Utah, there's one of the world's most incredible lakes: the Great Salt Lake. In the middle of the lake, there's an island: Antelope Island. In the middle of the island, there's a peak: Frary Peak. As soon as I saw it, I itched to stand at its summit.

Everything about the Great Salt Lake is immense. The clue is in the name. It currently measures around 75 miles long by 35 miles wide, although this varies. Historical records show that it has been both half as big and twice as big in the past, with the shoreline moving back and forth by as much as 15 miles. Seventeen thousand years ago, at its greatest extent, it was more than ten times as big. Known as Lake Bonneville, it then covered a third of what is now Utah. That must have been some sight.

Around the perimeter of the lake are enormous expanses of sands and salt flats. The blindingly white Bonneville Salt Flats in the west, covering an area of sixty square miles, are a world-famous venue for attempts on land speed records. At other points, mountainous peninsulas push deep into the water. The desert-like Promontory Mountains penetrate 20 miles and reach a height of 5,782ft. Ascents here are hot and rare. Some summits have probably never been trodden.

Antelope Island is the largest of several islands, measuring 15 miles long by 4.5 miles wide. From the 'mainland', near Salt Lake City, it can be reached by a 6.5ml causeway that carries a road. As my partner Sandi and I drove out into the lake across the narrow lifeline, it was as though we were being cast adrift from the security of the land. The island shimmered in the heat haze like a mirage, its skyline reflected on the bright surface of the lake, its shoreline merging with the still water so seamlessly that it was difficult to distinguish one from the other.

When we stopped to take a photograph, our senses were assailed by the smell of salt and the squawking of countless gulls. The lake is the second saltiest in the world after the Dead Sea. In places, it's ten times saltier than the oceans. Despite its salinity, it supports abundant life in the form of brine shrimp, brine flies and algae, which makes it a prime habitat for the millions of birds, over 250 species, that either live here or use it as a stopover during migration.

The island today is designated as a state park and is uninhabited, apart from a small day visitor centre overrun by a cacophony of martins. The few visitors who make the trip come to float in the waters or view the herd of more than 500 bison. These, together with bighorn sheep and the antelopes for which the first non-Native American explorers named the island in 1843, roam free and have little fear of humans. At one roadside halt, a coyote ambled past us without even a glance.

Frary Peak (6,596ft) is the highpoint on a broad ridge that climbs south from the visitor centre along the spine of the island. The route to the top is only 3.5 miles long, with an ascent of 2,100ft, but there's no shade or water to be had along the way. The trailhead sign warned that it was 'a strenuous hike with difficult terrain', and so it was to prove.

From the empty parking lot, the sun-baked trail climbed a

Frary Peak floats on the Great Salt Lake

scrubby hillside between gnarled outcrops of metamorphosed quartzite. Muted colours, heat haze and yellow mullein plants gave the scene an unreal sepia tone. The trail climbed over the ridge and continued along the far side, seeking the easiest route through fields of contorted rock formations.

Half a mile from the summit, it reached a hilltop radio tower on the ridge-crest and we saw the summit for the first time. It lay at the far end of a narrow, convoluted ridge, whose traverse required a hard and exposed scramble. After much deliberation, we couldn't summon up the will to tackle it in the debilitating heat. Most hikers who reach this point are of the same persuasion, for the trail avoids the ridge by dropping 60m/200ft below the crest and re-ascending close to the summit.

This alternative turned out to be no picnic either. With big drops below, the descent required care, while the re-ascent involved some awkward moves on steep, loose ground that had us scrabbling for tree roots. There used to be wooden steps here, but all that remains now is the half-buried rebar that used to support the crossboards. We were relieved to reach the small, tabletop summit.

The view was as extraordinary as is everything about the Great Salt Lake. To the east, the Wasatch Front of the Rocky

Mountains was an undifferentiated black skirting board on the horizon. Elsewhere, it was difficult to distinguish land from water. Dazzling, limitless brightness extended in all directions. This was a planet I no longer recognised. We were standing on a mountain that seemed to float unmoored on a sea of light. Never before had I felt such a sense of dislocation.

Then, of all things, it started to rain. The re-descent of the slippery rebar resulted in some undignified moves. The now grey sky merged with land and sea to add another surreal layer to the scene. We arrived back at the trailhead wet and bedraggled, though still sweating in the oppressive heat. Don't tell anyone I said so, but there are times when there is something to be said for a visitor centre with a cold drinks cabinet.

19

Red Faces on the Canyon Rim

WHEN THE Legend People were bad, Coyote turned them to stone and, at the place the Paiute call Angka-ku-wass-a-wits (The Place of the Red Painted Faces), they stand forever petrified, crumbling slowly in the desert sun. I hoped that the fate of the Legend People did not await me. Incorrigible as ever, I had entered a five-mile race at The Place of the Red Painted Faces, over 2,500m up in the Utah desert: the Bryce Canyon Rim Run.

The canyon consists of a 20-mile wall of cliffs that has been eroded into a vast rock amphitheatre. Within the bowl, the multi-coloured rock has been weathered into all sorts of fantastic walls and pinnacles. Teetering monoliths such as The Sentinel and Thor's Hammer rise hundreds of metres above their bases, while narrow canyons such as Wall Street burrow 500m deep between the formations to form virtually subterranean tunnels.

Some of the exquisitely sculpted pinnacles look uncannily lifelike. The more you stare at them, the more the Paiute legend explaining their origin seems credible. Elsewhere in Utah they are called stone babies, and to the national park rangers they are mysteriously known as hoodoos. Their spectacular colours come from minerals in the rock. Here you will find pink, orange and red blended with white, grey and cream, with occasional strips of lavender, pale yellow and brown. At dawn or sunset the canyon is an extraordinary and awesome sight, and it was here that I intended to run, along the rim of this fairyland of rock.

Now, I'm no runner. I've been known to bunny-hop down gentle hillsides and can semi-jog by leaning forward and willing my legs to keep up before I fall over. But a race? For which I was 'unacclimated' both for heat and altitude? Obviously, the challenge was too great to resist.

At 8am on race day, Ruby's Inn was a hive of activity. It was here, at the historic ranch on Bryce Canyon rim, that the adventure was to begin. 'Here's the man from Scotland,' announced the official who handed me my race number, and all at once I was the centre of attention. ET would not have attracted more curiosity. It was as if no one had ever seen a man from Scotland before, while the notion of an Englishman from Scotland was obviously going to be too complicated to explain. I could only hope I wasn't expected to run in a kilt. Being a standard bearer for my adopted country would only lead to disappointment for all concerned. There were 288 other runners and I would be content simply to complete the course.

'What altitude do you normally train at?' someone asked me.

'Train?' I thought. 'Zero,' I replied.

Along with my number I received a commemorative t-shirt, which I carefully folded and packed away in the car, saving it for bragging rights back home... should I survive.

My fellow competitors were from all age groups, from kids to supervets, and were evenly split between the sexes. The main objective seemed to be to have a good time, and that suited me fine. There was a carnival-like atmosphere as we assembled

beside the horse corrals and the petting place (where you can stroke tame goats).

And then we were off. Past a row of reconstructed Wild West buildings that included shops and a jail, past the building where you can buy ore and pan for gold, and out into the woods. It was a beautifully clear day, the sun had not yet risen high enough to make overheating a problem, and the altitude caused sweat to evaporate almost before it could form.

Bryce is officially classified as a 'Class 1' air quality area, with visibility often exceeding 100 miles, and the high, clean air was a joy to breathe. Despite the fact that I was soon struggling to inhale enough of it, the heady combination of thin air, striking scenery and sustained effort induced a trance-like state that made all the pain disappear. It was a phenomenon I have experienced on several disparate occasions, when the desire to savour a once-in-a-lifetime experience, to take in every sight, sound and smell, overcomes any physical discomfort.

The route led along forest trails through quaking aspen trees to the canyon rim, where a large pocket of hoodoos appeared below. We thinned out into a long line, a ribbon of humanity caught between the crumbling red abyss below and the achingly

ECCENTRIC ESCAPADES

blue sky overhead. Gradually the route climbed uphill and for once there were more red faces on the canyon rim than there were among the hoodoos.

The trail eventually looped downhill again and levelled off through such beautifully dappled woodland that I didn't want it to end. I crossed the finish line in 39 minutes 36 seconds. Eight-minute miles may be a tad short of Olympian standard but, like I said, I'm no runner. I felt elated. The marshall who took my number wore a stetson and only needed a silver star to look like Wyatt Earp. 'How're ya doin', Ralph?' he asked. Throughout my life, I'd always wondered if my '15 minutes of fame' would ever arrive, and here it was.

After recovering my breath, I moseyed across to a row of tables piled high with freshly cut melons and oranges – now that's a sight you don't see at the end of the London marathon. In the now hot sun, the juice-heavy fruit tasted exquisite. No less than 72 medals were awarded, three for each of 12 age groups for each sex. I managed to avoid one by coming sixth in my own group. The male winner clocked 26.58, while the top woman was fifth in 28.44.

The medal ceremony was preceded and followed by a country and western singer and a cowboy poet who told the tale of how the first Bryce Rim Run took place when Adam chased Eve through the canyon. How he managed to rhyme 'Eve' with 'fig leaf' is still a mystery to me. A free lunch ended the morning's festivities, but all runners were offered free tickets to the evening's rodeo. I declined.

Back on the familiar hills of home, I often recall my Bryce Canyon Rim Run with fondness. I bask in the knowledge that I am the fastest ever (if only) British entrant and, as I'd hoped, the envy on the faces of my walking companions when I don my t-shirt is usually sufficient to sustain me for another mile or two.

20

Canyoneering in Utah

THE FOOT WASN'T designed to take up residence adjacent to the head. It's affixed to the bottom of the leg for a reason. If there's any business required up top, that's what hands are for.

I had pause to consider these fundamentals of human anatomy during an ascent of Peek-a-Boo Canyon in the Escalante region of southern Utah. It's where canyoneers go when they die and go to heaven. Canyon*eers*, note. Some Brits refer to canyoneering as canyoning, but the Americans have it right. As with mountains, where I mountain*eer*, so with canyons.

There are canyons in other parts of the world, even in the UK, but they're nothing like the canyons of Utah. British canyoneering tends to consist mostly of mooching along a riverbed in cold water between vegetated banks. Things are different over the Pond. The soft sandstone of the southwest was specifically made to be weathered by the elements into all kinds of fantastical shapes, and this has produced a natural playground for a whole host of recreational pursuits.

Harder rock stands proud and tall, forming the buttes and mesas familiar to any fan of John Ford westerns. Softer rock has been gouged out by stream action to form deep fissures or 'slot canyons' that are sometimes hundreds of feet deep. Most are dry, although after rain 'flash floods' can rapidly fill them to the brim. Some harbour permanent deep pools that need to be swum. Some require rock climbing technique to penetrate. Some are so narrow that they are accessible only to very thin people or not at all.

Eddies of long-disappeared water have sculpted the rock into a variety of beautiful natural features whose intricacy compares with that found in the interior of complex caves. The walls often overlap as they spiral and intertwine above you, like a double helix of DNA. Their mineral-rich rainbow colours are famously photogenic when hit by the sun. Exploring such convoluted places is a cross between scrambling and caving, but in the dry, in the daylight and with zero exposure.

Peek-a-Boo is only one slot canyon among thousands hidden in the complex drainage of the Escalante River system, which is itself only one of many vast river systems. Through-hiking source-canyons requires multi-day trips with packs, and leaves you a long way from your starting point, often with no easy way back, so this is a specialised activity. More accessible side canyons like Peek-a-Boo are shorter and can be combined with others (up one and down the other) to make a round trip.

Peek-a-Boo's main draw is its challenging nature. Imagine a sunken series of interlinked potholes, tunnelling through a procession of overhead arches, lined by swirling fins of rock that overlap and seem to close off the route ahead. Although the narrows are only around half a mile long, they take as long to negotiate as would a rock climb of that length. Yet no rope work is required. As you never leave the canyon floor, you can't fall. The through-trip is technically no more than a strenuous scramble... but in magical surroundings. It brings back latent memories of what it was like as a child to discover an exciting new playground.

For Sandi and I, even reaching the canyon was an adventure, courtesy of a 26-mile rattle along a dirt track known as Hole-in-the-Rock Road. We arrived at a dusty parking lot, unsurprised to find that our rental car was the only two-wheel-drive vehicle there. A path led down through sand and scrub into Dry Fork Wash and the entrance to Peek-a-Boo, a disconcerting six metres up the wall of the sun-baked wash. Holds had been cut into the rock to facilitate access, so we duly scrambled up and inserted ourselves into the canyon mouth.

The potholes that floored the canyon were more in the nature of saucer-shaped hollows than deep pits. Progress was made by heaving yourself up and over the back rim of one into the bowl of the next higher one. The rock was water-smoothed,

Peek-a-Boo promenade

with few holds and little purchase, so fingers, elbows and knees were soon grazed.

Sometimes the next pothole was only a few feet higher. Sometimes it was high enough to require a mantelshelf. And sometimes we had to flail and squirm over the rim in an avalanche of arms and legs and slither into the hollow on our stomachs. As a bonus, this at least enabled me to take compromising shots of Sandi that I could later use as bargaining chips.

The most awkward obstacle was a short, inclined rock chute that curved upwards around a tight hairpin bend between walls that were barely a body-width apart. Inserting head and shoulders around the bend was no problem, but then there were no handholds and no purchase for the feet from which to launch oneself further upwards around the corner against the friction of the rock.

Somehow, by some mode of locomotion that remains a mystery to me, I managed to force my way up in a frenzy of grunts and groans that echoed around the enclosed space.

Graciously, I deigned to give Sandi a helping hand up after me. But it was she who was to have the last laugh...

The canyon walls decreased in height and we climbed out into the parched desert. We had 'hiked' Peek-a-Boo, but now we had to get back. The standard return route, to prolong the fun, is to make a round trip by descending nearby Spooky Canyon, which was supposed to be less strenuous.

After chimneying down into the upper slot, it turned out to be one of those canyons best suited to short, thin people. The floor was sandy and mostly level, devoid of any difficulty, but the gap between the walls was less than body width and allowed only sideway passage – a claustrophobe's nightmare. Sandi is shorter than me and managed to squeeze her way along in crablike fashion, but my head would not fit in the narrow space above where hers had passed through. Nor was there sufficient room between the walls, in a sideways position, to bend the knees and crouch down.

While she raced ahead (or so it seemed to me), I side-shuffled back to a slight widening where I could shimmy down to the ground and slither along the floor, pushing my rucksack ahead of me.

I emerged blinking into desert heat to find Sandi standing hands on hips, feigning impatience but grinning from ear to ear. We paused to suck the last drops of moisture from our water bottles then hightailed it back to the car to indulge in some full-on a/c... and search the guidebook for another fix.

21

Tatraneering For All

SATURDAY MORNING in the village of Lysa Polana on the Polish side of the Tatra Range, the highest mountains between the Alps and the Caucasus. The year is 1991 – the first summer following the fall of the Berlin Wall. There are still frontier guards with Kalashnikovs on the Cuillin-like Tatra spine, which separates Poland from Czechoslovakia (as the country was called before Slovakia decoupled from the Czech Republic in 1993). Poles who climb to the main ridge are still nervous about taking baby steps over the border, but the joy of being able to do so is palpable on their faces.

Back down in Lysa Polana, it is as though this normally sleepy border town has succumbed to a popular invasion. South of the town, a human tide washes up the road towards the mountains, from toddlers in harness to old-timers limping with walking sticks, from heavily laden backpackers (mostly from western Europe) to families dressed in their Sunday best. All are out of breath but move continuously, perhaps trying to keep up with the inhuman Polish guidebook times.

Overloaded horse-drawn carts carry those who do not wish to walk and can afford to pay for a ride. No cars are allowed on the road. A passenger hanging off the back of a cart gets his foot caught in the wheel and is carried away on someone's back. A horse slips and falls under the weight of its load. A group of girls form a chorus line as they sing and dance up the road. Everyone is happy.

Where are these people going? They are making the five-miles-long trek to a lake called Morskie Oko, the Eye of the Sea. It is a grand lake, the largest in the Tatra and 50m deep, said to be linked underground with the sea and bottomed with sunken ships. Surrounding the lake is an amphitheatre of some of the highest, most spectacular and curiously named peaks in the High Tatra. Peaks such as the teetering Mnich (the Monk), its shadowing twin Zadni Mnich (Hind Monk), abie Sczcyty (Frog Peak), abia Lalka (Frog Doll) and Rysy, whose 2,499m north summit is the highest point in Poland.

What lures all these people to the Tatra? Poland's troubled past is little known in the UK, apart perhaps from Hitler's invasion of 1939. At one time or another over the centuries, the country has been invaded by whichever European state was the temporary superpower. For the whole of the 19th century, it was partitioned between Austria, Prussia and Russia and disappeared from the map altogether until reinstated following World War One in 1918. Throughout this turbulent history, the Tatra, in the words of a local guidebook, 'soared above the tormented country like a torch of freedom'. It was here, in the remote valleys, that the flame of independence was kept alight.

Polish symphony orchestras still play Zygmunt Noskowski's 1875 Morskie Oko Symphony. The poet Franciszek Henryk Siła-Nowicki described the mountains as altars of freedom in a giant natural cathedral. The scientist Stanisław Staszic climbed Lomnicky (2,634m), and in a widely read speech declared: 'You, the lasting monuments for generations to come, raised to inaccessible heights and digging your peaks into the clouds; you will preserve the undying name of the Poles.' Lomnicky, in what is now Slovakia, was then thought to be the highest Tatra, but that honour was later claimed by Gerlachovsky (2,655m).

The scenes on the road to Morskie Oko are startling enough to western eyes, but what happens beyond there is even more remarkable. For many, the lake is only a brief stop en route to an attempt on Rysy itself, nearly ten miles from and 1,500m above Lysa Polana.

At the beginning of each summer, the Chief of TANAP, the Polish mountain rescue service, makes his customary annual appeal to all and sundry to take care on the hill. The message falls on deaf ears. No one carries a map, very few have rucksacks. Those who have anything worth carrying put it in a shopping bag and sling it over their shoulder. No one wears anything resembling what in Britain would be thought of as hillwalking gear. Men wear denim jeans, women sometimes wear their everyday skirts.

On their feet they wear decrepit trainers, even on limestone peaks such as Giewont, where the rock is very slippery when wet. No one carries survival equipment or even much food or water. Foul-weather gear consists of a plastic mac or a plastic bag to cover the head.

A short ramble on Rysy

The path above Morskie Oko is paved with large boulders and climbs straight up the mountainside like a staircase. It's incredibly hard on the knees and so crowded that, in the unlikely event of anyone having the energy to do so, overtaking is virtually impossible. The path climbs 200m to Czarny Staw (Black Lake) then makes a directissima ascent of a gully at the back. At this pace it's tough work but no-one stops for a breather for more than a few seconds. Onwards and upwards the stair-case rises but, just when you think you're getting somewhere, things really begin to happen.

The path reaches the foot of a long rock rib that curves up beside an imposing cliff face. It's like Curved Ridge on Buachaille Etive Mor in Glen Coe. And now you're clambering on outwardly sloping rock with few handholds above appreciable exposure. Much of it is a straightforward scramble, but some moves would be graded at least a Moderate rock climb in the UK and would daunt many a walker. Not in Poland. No one here seems to have any conception that it is possible to fall. No one appears to countenance failure, no matter what their age, ability or dress. No one even slows down.

ECCENTRIC ESCAPADES

In some places the rock becomes so steep that the holds run out and it is necessary to haul yourself up free-hanging chains, Tarzan-fashion. No one turns back. No one looks scared.

A woman slips to near the edge, regains her footing and continues at the same relentless pace. We pass a father who takes his young daughter by the hand and dangles her down an exposed rock step until her feet touch the ledge below. A young boy descends another section of vertical rock by sliding down a fixed chain while his father watches and offers advice and I have to look away.

Mid-afternoon. The ascent continues. No one carries a torch. What will these people do when it gets dark? I can't say, because I didn't make the summit. My colleague Ali was waiting for me down at Morskie Oko and I'd used up my allotted ascent time. I was loath to turn back, but gathering cloud, together with a glimpse of the summit still disconcertingly high above, made the decision easier to bear.

In the days that followed, I learned that the carefree Polish approach to hillwalking I had witnessed on Rysy was unexceptional. A few incidents in particular are etched into my memory. On the slippery rocks of Giewont (1,895m), cloud whipped across the summit and the rain sheeted down mercilessly, yet a queue of people waited patiently to climb the final chains to a summit so cramped that it seemed any new arrival must displace someone down the far side.

Out of the snow-swirling mist on Kasprowy Wierch (1,985m), a figure appears. It turns out to be a woman wearing flat court shoes and a skirt and wielding an umbrella against the wind. And the most indelible image of all, on the Orla Perc (Eagle's Way), the hardware-festooned route along the sharp Tatra spine… A conga-line of people descend chains, pinned to a blank rock wall, into the deep V-shaped slot known as Kozia Przełęcz (Goat's Pass). A queue forms at the top of a final, vertical five-metre ladder as a party of nuns dressed in flowing black habits and flip-flops take it in turns to descend from rung to rung.

The delight with which these ill-equipped 'hillwalkers' take to the hills is infectious. Yes, there are accidents – helicopter pilots log a lot of flight time during a Tatra summer. But who would deny the right of these people, who live in an achingly flat country, to enjoy their *montagnes de poche* (as the French call them) in whichever way they choose?

Having been raised in the safety-first British hillwalking tradition, I could never climb in such a high-risk way, but I do not judge. On the contrary, I admire, applaud, even envy the matter-of-fact audaciousness of a nation in which no one turns a head at the sight of nuns in flip-flops cavorting gaily on a high rock face.

Misguided Misadventures

22

Blood Trails of Greece

IN WOODY ALLEN'S film *Bananas*, he is shocked to find himself wounded. 'Blood!' he cries. 'That should be on the inside!' I had cause to reflect on this revelation when I tried to climb a mountain in Greece.

After an incident-packed hitch-hike across Europe in the late 1960s, I fetched up in Saloniki (Thessalonica) in northern Greece. Penniless and undernourished from days on the road, I was in no position to reach any of the mountains further south, or to climb them even if I could reach them.

There was a convenient solution to the problem, as I learned when I checked in at the local youth hostel: sell my blood. As in many other countries, blood donation in Greece was (and still is) insufficient to cover transfusion needs. To make up the difference, some has to be imported, but for an emergency transfusion it may be left to the friends and relatives of the patient to locate donors. Where to look for willing subjects in need of cash? By chance, I was staying in donor central.

Those lucky enough to posses rare A or B blood types could barter for considerable sums. Even a common-or-garden O+ like myself, given a simple diet, could live for a week off the going rate for a half-litre. In the corridors of the hostel I passed pale, zombie-like creatures, with arms like pin cushions, who existed by selling two half-litres a week. In the UK, the minimum donation interval for a male is 12 weeks.

Larger sums of blood money were available in Istanbul further east, but the Saloniki grapevine advised caution. There were horror stories, hopefully apocryphal, about having to put your arm through a hole in the wall so that you couldn't see how much blood was being taken, and of bodies being found drained in the Bosphorus. It was perhaps fortunate for me that Turkey lay off-route.

The donation procedure at the local Saloniki hospital was as straightforward as in the UK, except that instead of a cup of tea in exchange for a half-litre of the life-giving red plasma, you received a sum of cash. In pre-euro days, this amounted to several hundred drachma. I've never earned money so quickly and easily.

After re-emerging into the cauldron of a Greek summer afternoon, I took what I thought would be an easy stroll up to the ancient walls that surround the city, only to discover that even a climb of a few hundred feet defeated me. Weak and dizzy, I blew a good proportion of my earnings on salty snacks and iced drinks.

Days later, I'd made it down to Athens and another hostel. In the middle of the night, the dorm was woken by cries of 'O positive'. Sleepily, as though commanded, those of us with the requisite blood type filed out to be ferried down to the hospital. Another poor accident victim might need us and, in truth, I was more than willing to go. The money would again be welcome and, after long days on the road, at the beck and call of indifferent motorists, it felt good to be wanted, if only for my blood.

After another half-litre had been siphoned from my body, for the second time in a week, I rose to my feet and collapsed in a heap. I awoke on a hospital bed to find a swarthy man advancing towards me. With unconcealed disdain, he tossed a wad of drachma in my general direction. I may have been saving the life of his relative, but we donors were still viewed as mercenary scum. My blood-selling days were over.

The Greek mainland is a chunky peninsula that runs southeast from Albania between the Adriatic Sea and the Aegean Sea.

Its spine is a continuous range of mountains that includes numerous 2,000m peaks and five 2,500m peaks, the highest of which is 2,917m Mount Olympus. Although not high by world standards, they are more than twice the height of UK mountains, while great gorges and inadequate roads hinder access. Add to that a lack of guidebooks and maps, and climbing any Greek mountain was going to be an ambitious endeavour. I hoped to make use of local knowledge.

My objective was one of the 2,500m peaks, of which the easiest to reach was Mount Parnassus (2,547m). A good road ran from Athens to Delphi at its foot and, from there, a 2,000m climb would put me at the summit. It would be a long day out, but no more so than several I'd done in the Highlands.

In the event, none of that mattered. By the time I'd reached Delphi, I was as pale as the living dead I'd met in Saloniki. Taking a day out to see the archaeological sights, I could barely make it up the short path to the Temple of Apollo, just above town. In those days access to the temple was still permitted, so I sat down in the shade of one of the five remaining pillars, my back against the cool stone, and barely moved all day. As the sun crossed the sky, I merely shifted position to remain in the pillar's shadow.

Delphi is the site of Greece's most famous oracle, where the god Apollo spoke through a sibyl (priestess) to supplicants. I had no need to consult her. Her most famous maxim, carved into the temple, was insight enough. *Know Thyself.* I had learned that there were limits to what I could put my body through. It was a salutary lesson.

Mount Parnassus remained out of reach.

I have still to climb *any* mountain on the Greek mainland.

23

Seconds Away

WHEN ROGER PEELED into the air and landed beside me with a thud, I should have realised we weren't cut out to be rock jocks. It was our first attempt at rock climbing. If I'd believed in fate, I would have given up there and then.

Red Craig, Glen Clova. A training ground for Dundee climbers and an initiation rite for beginners. Experienced rock climber Alec showed us how to tie on to the rope and led us, one at a time, up 'Twenty Minute Mod'. No rock climb is more calculated to infuse beginners with confidence. We were well aware that Moderate was the lowest grade in the climbing world's hierarchy of difficulty, but the ease with which we romped up it had us salivating for more. Difficult, Very Difficult, Severe, Very Severe... surely they couldn't be *that* much harder?

Alec's second top rope disabused us of our naïvety. Hanging Chimney (Severe) was well named. In the struggle to heave myself up its tight confines against the pull of gravity, it was indeed possible just to hang there with one's feet dangling over space. The outcome was seriously in doubt until a heart-bursting thrutch popped me out the top.

Alec next offered one of us the opportunity to lead the easier Larch Tree Wall (Very Difficult). Both Roger and I were keen and exchanged pleading looks. I let him have the honour. To this day, I wonder what would have happened had he deferred to me instead.

It began to drizzle. Roger climbed 30 or 40 feet. He reached the crux. The rope stopped paying out. He fell. If it hadn't been for the sloping ground at the foot of the climb, which lessened the shock of the impact, there might have been a worse outcome for him than a broken wrist and a transient pallor.

Neither Roger nor I were destined to become great rock

Classic abseiling on the Cuillin Ridge '60s-style (no harness, no abseil device)

climbers but, unlike him, I persevered. I was determined that lack of technical ability would not curb my freedom of the hills.

Over the years, this has led me into a variety of scrapes, which I have so far survived, occasionally through skill or experience, more often through luck or cowardice. In *The Joy of Hillwalking* I describe how, on Buachaille Etive Mor in Glen Coe, my leader fell, the piton to which I was belayed came out and we both pendulumed across the exposed face of Rannoch Wall, swinging from a precarious running belay he'd had the foresight to place.

In the misleadingly named Little Gully in the Cuillin of Skye, my own painstakingly placed runner somehow managed to slip off a rock flake, and I found myself unprotected on a long run out as I backed nervously up through the roof window of the crux cave pitch. On Dairsie Crag in Fife, I abseiled down the rock face without problem. When Robin followed immediately afterwards, the belay gave way and he plunged 20 feet into a gorse bush. A bit of elbow bone disappeared inside his arm and the doctors were unable to find it. As on Larch Tree Wall, it could have been me.

Surprisingly, it wasn't such incidents that began to erode my desire to rock climb. It was Richard. Richard was a fine rock climber but he couldn't muster the patience for it. For him, it was a slow activity made even slower by gear management and brought to a halt by the need to stand around belaying. He wanted to move. While I'd spend the day hanging around on some rock face, he'd take an easier, perhaps even more interesting, way to the summit, stroll from top to top along some scenic ridge and return glowing. To my chagrin, I was envious. My route was a detail on the mountain. He ranged.

It made me reconsider why I climbed mountains, and I had to admit that tramping the tops held greater appeal than working my way up a rock face with a big drop beneath my feet. I wasn't a thrill seeker. I wanted to get high.

Rock climbing for me has consequently rarely been an end in itself, more a means to an end. But I do understand the appeal.

I have felt the exhilaration that comes from three-dimensional problem solving and gravity-defying movement on steep rock. Perhaps if I'd been a better rock climber, or a better thrill seeker, I would have pushed my limits further. But I am neither. If I ever get the chance to climb Everest, it will be by the easiest route, and I don't mind if there are fixed ropes to help me past the tricky bits.

Or perhaps it all stems from Roger's fall. Or Richard's attitude. Roger and Richard. It's their fault.

24

Going Underground

THERE ARE TOO many mountains in the world to climb in a single lifetime. There are even too many in the UK for most. Of those who seek to climb Scotland's 282 Munros, only a small minority manage to bag the whole lot.

For most of us, time away from the 9–5 is limited. Weekends and holidays are precious. Choices have to be made. That's where a guidebook comes in. I want to know the best places to go.

On the other hand, I love to explore. I envy the pioneers of old, for whom every trip into the mountains broke new ground in a way that's no longer possible today. Roads, upland vehicle tracks, man-made paths, fences, pylons, wind farms, crowds... even without a guidebook, it's hardly undiscovered country.

There are still places in the UK, especially in Scotland, where you can get 'off the beaten track' and discover secret places you're sure no one has visited before. But there's only one place left to do *real* exploration, where you have no idea what to expect or what lies around the next corner, and that's underground. This holds true even if you use a guidebook, because cave interiors are generally too dark and complex to describe in useful detail.

It was only a few years ago, in 2011, that caves in Cumbria, Lancashire and Yorkshire were linked to form England's longest system. At the time of writing, it has no less than 55 miles of passages, with further extensions probable in the future. But how many people have even heard of the Three Counties System?

The longest cave in Wales is the 43-miles-long Ogof Draenen, while Ireland's longest is the ten-miles-long Pollnagollum–Poulelva cave in County Clare. Plenty of room for exploration there. Compared to such underground riches, Scotland is hard done by. The longest Scottish cave is the Uamh an Claonaite in the Northern Highlands, where years of sump diving have so far yielded only two miles of hard-won passage.

The most well-known caves in Scotland are sea caves such as Smoo Cave on the north coast and Fingal's Cave on the Isle of Staffa. Like most caves of their ilk, they have little length beyond their huge entrances. Long passages are found only in extensive beds of limestone, which Scotland conspicuously lacks. The limestone caves that do exist are characterised by hard-to-find entrances backed by cramped crawl ways. They provide energetic sport.

Exploring such hidey-holes demands of the caver the flexibility of a contortionist and the stickability of a mud wrestler. I lack both accomplishments but am thankfully unafflicted by what for many is a speleological deal breaker: claustrophobia. To me, the blackness beyond the reach of the torch beam gives a sense of limitless space, because there is no end to what you can see. Outside that beam of light might as well be infinity.

Despite my limitations, my desire for exploration ensured that it was only a matter of time before I was lured underground. In Kingston Master Cave in the Yorkshire Dales, a short ladder pitch led to a large stream passage along which we splashed like carefree children. In Bruntscar Cave, a roomy passage led to waterfalls whose negotiation was more fun than any waterpark feature.

But increasingly, as though egged on by some devilish imp perched on my shoulder, I was strangely drawn to the more esoteric pleasures of the awkward, unsung caves of Scotland.

A roomy section of the Cave of the Knives

Thrutching one's way through their confined spaces was never going to be easy, but it was also never going to be less than interesting. Given my penchant for idiosyncratic adventure, I should perhaps have foreseen that it would land me in a whole new set of predicaments for which I was singularly ill prepared.

The Uamh an Sgeinne (Cave of the Knives) is a typically constricted Skye cave. The entrance is a small letterbox opening in an inconspicuous rock outcrop hidden on a remote hillside. Behind the entrance, a short tube descends to a prolonged crawl whose crux is a jack-knifing squeeze around an awkward stal column.

Not far beyond here, Jim and I turned back when we reached a tight tube half-filled with water. It was his first trip underground and, for some reason, despite his prior enthusiasm, the actuality was failing to fill him with exploratory zeal. His conviction that this was an aberrant and undignified pursuit for an adult was reinforced by an unfortunate incident that he later confessed had him wondering whether he would ever see daylight again.

Both our head torches went out.

At the same time.

With no backup (a lesson well and truly learned), we found ourselves in complete darkness, and I do mean complete. Underground darkness isn't like nighttime darkness. In the blackness of a cave, you can't even see your hand in front of your face. Finding a way out of a complex cave in such circumstances is almost impossible. All rocks, nooks and crannies feel the same. Working your way around a perimeter, as you might to find the door in a dark room, won't work because you'll most likely miss the one small hole that may be the sole key to the exit route. And you'll soon lose your bearings anyway.

While Jim attempted to quell the rising panic that his voice betrayed, I set my mind to solving the problem. Surely not both light bulbs and both sets of batteries could have failed at the same time. Carefully, very carefully, *extremely* carefully, I dismantled both torches on my lap. I placed each separate item in a precise location, so that I could find it again by touch alone, and swapped the batteries. The possibility of a dropped battery was an eventuality I refused to contemplate.

At length, I managed to piece together a single operational torch that re-illuminated both our exit route and Jim's distress. I handed him the torch for reassurance and he scampered off like a rat, leaving me in his wake. I had to call him back before he was out of earshot.

Jim never ventured down a cave again, but the desire to see around the next corner has led me back down into that underground world of darkness again and again. Usually, there has been nothing around the next corner except another corner... but who knows what may lie around that? There may be a stream, a waterfall, a large cavern or a beautiful stal formation. And once, just once, there was a new passage that no one had noticed before...

25

The Plughole Extension

AS I WAS NEVER destined to be a rock climber, I was never destined to be a speleologist. Yet I have persevered with both beyond the level of competence, and this has led me into some exceptional situations. On one extraordinary occasion, it fell to me by chance to discover the holy grail of all speleology: new passage. It was the only time in my life, up to now, about which I can truly say that I undertook some real exploration, when I was able to go where no one had gone before.

In the depths of any known cave, it is unusual to find a new passage that no one has noticed before. Usually there is none. If there is any, its entrance may begin as a minute hole, or be hidden behind a rock, or be blocked by silt... or all three. But for anyone who finds it, it is akin to finding a new mountain. In the whole history of the human race, you are the first to go there, the first even to see it. It's the draw of exploration.

Poll Seomar (Chamber Pot) is a 20m-deep hole on an Argyll hillside. The guidebook had nothing interesting to say about it. Paul and I lounged beside the entrance, already exhausted from adventures in nearby caves such as the Cave of the Roaring Waters and the Cave of the Skulls. My companion seemed content simply to collect the magic mushrooms that carpeted the ground roundabout. On a whim, I roused him to action. The Pot appeared to offer a nice and easy descent to round off a good day's exploration before we headed home.

We scrambled down without incident but, at the bottom, purely by chance, I noticed a hole behind a boulder. Instinctively, I inserted myself into it feet first. A few moments later, I shimmied out onto a wide, sloping bedding plane. It descended away from me, barely a couple of feet high, roofed with pencil-thin stalactites that almost touched the rock floor on which I was lying. As the stalactites barred the way forward, it was obvious that I had entered a new cave, but the significance of the discovery was overshadowed by my eagerness to see what lay beyond.

I squirmed my way down the rock floor, taking as narrow a line as possible through the stalactites. Regrettably, some snapped and tinkled down as I passed. Despite taking as much care as possible, there was no way to avoid all of them.

At the foot of the slope, a small stream came in from the right. To the left, it disappeared down a gently sloping tube large enough to crawl along on hands and knees. I pushed on into the bowels of the earth, barely able to believe that no one had passed this way before. At one point, a dry passage, like an oxbow bend, took a brief detour. Cupped in the corner of the bend was a small grouping of larger stalactites and stalagmites that would later see the Chamber Pot re-rated as one of the most decorated in Argyll.

Now I could hear the distant roar of a huge waterfall, echoing up the passage like an underground Niagara. I approached with quickening pulse, only to laugh at my own foolishness when I reached it. The stream tumbled down a drop in the passage of no more than a couple of feet. The sound had been heightened by the confined space. Not far beyond here, the stream disappeared into gravel and the passage came to an end.

But that wasn't the end of the excitement. Paul arrived soon after me. In our eagerness to see where the passage had been leading us, we'd taken insufficient care to note the route. On the way back out, at the top of the bedding plane, we reached a dead end. The hole back up to the bottom of the Chamber Pot simply wasn't there any longer. All around us was solid rock.

Instinctively, we looked at each other. Later, we would both express relief that we could detect no sign of panic in the other's eyes. There was a problem. We would have to work together to solve it. Panic would not help.

It was a turning point in our relationship. Before the trip, we had been more acquaintances than friends, but in that reassuring

Where no one has gone before

glance a permanent bond was formed. In that instant of adversity, like roped climbers who suddenly find that their lives depend on each other, we became more than companions. We became trusted friends.

Painstakingly, we inched our way back along the passage, searching every nook and cranny for an opening. Eventually we found the exit hole and managed to worm our way back up into daylight.

We retired to a hostelry to replenish our reserves and mull over our adventure. We decided that, until we had an opportunity to investigate further, the new cave must remain a secret. A few months later, we went back. As we approached the passage end, I was taken aback when my torch beam caught the impression of a boot in the mud. In our absence, someone else had found our new passage! Then I realised that it was my own bootprint, undisturbed from our previous visit. A permanent mark.

We intended to explore the cave further, even attempt to survey it, but better cavers than us found their way in and our brief encounter with exploration glory was over. At least, as the discoverers of the new passage, we got to name it. It exited the bottom of the Chamber Pot, so we called it the Plughole Extension. The bedding plane we named Stal Mall. We still haven't got around to naming the other parts. It's an ongoing project. These are important matters.

Like I say, I was never destined to be a speleologist, but that only made my discovery of the Plughole Extension an even more remarkable event. I still find it hard to believe that a novice such as myself was granted the privilege of blundering his way into new passage. I was the first. No one, *no one*, can ever take that away from me.

26

Snowbound in Wartime

SPRINGTIME IN THE Scottish Highlands is the most Alpine time of the year, when glistening snow still caps the peaks but has retreated from approach paths. In 1982, the white stuff lay later than usual. With a Bank Holiday Monday opening up a three-day weekend window, it seemed an ideal time to climb Beinn na Lap. The 935m elongated pimple could never be considered beautiful, but its unique situation makes it a real prize.

It lies in the middle of the roadless wilderness that stretches for some 50 miles between the west coast and the Cairngorms. A day hike is out of the question and the summit would be difficult to reach at all were it not for the presence of a remote railway station, the only one on the British rail network inaccessible by road, near its foot. In those days, Corrour Halt, as it is now known, was manned, but there was nothing else there but the stationmaster's house.

The railway timetable still made access awkward for those of us who worked five-day weeks because, in those days, there were no Sunday trains. Hence the necessity for a Monday holiday to enable a three-day visit.

On Saturday 1 May, Christine and I alighted at Corrour and watched the train disappear from sight, leaving us alone on the empty platform. All was silence and wilderness. The lifeline to civilisation had been cut. Whatever happened now, we were on our own.

We lugged camping gear to a pitch near Loch Ossian at the foot of Beinn na Lap and settled in for what turned out to be an uncomfortable night. The temperature unexpectedly dropped well below zero and our three-season sleeping bags struggled to cope. In the morning, we found that the water we had brought for breakfast had frozen in the water bottles.

At eight o'clock it still seemed eerily dark. Shivering, I unzipped the fly, climbed out of the tent and emerged into the mother of all storms. Overnight the land had been transformed. In all my years in the Highlands, I have never known so much snow fall overnight. Maybe a couple of feet. It was difficult to tell because the texture was light and fluffy, with huge flakes, almost honeycombed, like cotton wool.

The gale that had brought the snow lashed our flimsy summer tent and blew horizontal snow across the moor, producing whiteout conditions. I squinted into the spindrift. Not only could I not see Beinn na Lap, I couldn't even see Loch Ossian. A layer of snow had built up on the flysheet, which explained why it was dark inside. I let it lie, for insulation, packed snow around the flysheet hem for added security, and dived back in.

It was immediately obvious that any attempt to climb Beinn na Lap was out of the question. We might have considered retreating to Corrour, except that there was no Sunday train. We were well and truly snowbound in the wilderness. Warmth eluded us, even in our sleeping bags.

Rather than freeze in the tent, we decided to attempt to climb Meall na LIce, a minor hill top only 583m high and less than 200m above us. It was to be the most exhausting little climb either of us had ever made. The snow was freakish. It was so unconsolidated that it was impossible to walk on top of it, yet attempting to push through it merely compressed it in front until it blocked further movement.

The only way to progress was to raise one's foot high and sink it further forward until it touched the ground beneath. In places, the snow was so deep that it was necessary to use a hand to raise the boot clear of the snow, which resulted in a variety of acrobatic tumbles but limited hilarity. To avoid the constant falling over, we even resorted to crawling on hands and knees. This, despite facefuls of spindrift from being so close to the ground. It was hard to believe it was May.

Reluctant to be beaten by a paltry 200m ascent, we persevered and reached the summit plateau. Now we were faced by a band of snowdrift so deep that it presented an almost impassable barrier. When I stepped onto it, it gave way like quicksand. I sank to my chest. With my feet having touched solid ground, I made progress by leaning forward and making swimming motions with my arms, doggy-paddle style.

The summit itself lay hidden beneath us somewhere and was impossible to locate. All attempts to do so were soon abandoned anyway, courtesy of the arrival of a new force of nature...

Suddenly, eerily, the mist illuminated, as though the brightness control had been turned up to dazzling. The roar of thunder that followed closely, too closely, behind the flash of lightning seemed to make even the snow tremble. Without further need for deliberation, we flung ourselves downhill in a tangle of limbs and arrived back at the tent soaked to the skin.

The second night at Loch Ossian was warmer – much warmer. We awoke on the Monday to find that most of the snow had disappeared as quickly as it had arrived, as though it had been a figment of our imaginations. The gale was still howling, though, so we struck camp and fought our way to the station to catch the early train out. As it approached out of the swirling mist, it seemed to us a lifesaver. No railway carriage had ever felt more luxurious. As the engine battled the gale in our stead, we lounged in cocooned warmth and drank reviving cups of steaming tea.

But the biggest shock of the weekend was still to come. It was Monday 3 May 1982. While we had been away, the Falklands crisis, sparked by Argentina's invasion of the British islands, had escalated into a full-scale fire-fight. We learned that on Saturday a British Vulcan bomber had bombed Port Stanley airfield. On Sunday the British naval task force had sunk the nuclear submarine *General Belgrano* with the loss of over 300 men. On Tuesday the British destroyer HMS *Sheffield* would be sunk and a Harrier jump jet shot down. While we had been away, our country had gone to war.

It was hard to process this information. I'd thought I was coming back to civilisation, but there is nothing civilised about war. A shared battle against the elements would surely convince anyone that cooperation is a more fruitful strategy for solving problems than conflict.

Perhaps the human condition, being the product of evolution through nature 'red in tooth and claw', makes confrontation inevitable. But fresh out of the wilderness, it was hard to see human aggression as anything other than ridiculous. As I re-entered 'civilisation' from the snows, I came up with a solution that I was sure would resolve 99 per cent of confrontation scenarios: stop fighting and go take a hike!

27

Icefall Shenanigans

SANDY WAS A MUCH better climber than I was, and I don't mean to damn him by faint praise. It was thanks to his skill and determination that, much to my surprise, I found myself tackling winter routes on the North Face of Ben Nevis. In the great Scottish tradition, he was drawn to climb in conditions most of us might consider hazardous even for festering in a tent. The more the buttresses bulged with ice and the gullies brimmed with snow, the more he loved it. Battling against nightfall and/or blizzard was a bonus.

He trusted me as his second on the rope and I was eager to learn. New to Scottish winter mountaineering, ignorant of danger, imbued with the immortality of youth, I trusted him to lead me to places I would never have ventured otherwise. If he was willing to lead, I was willing to follow. What could possibly go wrong?

Oddly, in my early days on the hill, I was never as tentative on snow and ice as I was on rock. Even more oddly, despite all evidence to the contrary, this is still the case. My head tells me that rock is generally reliable and secure, whereas ice is a tad slippery. My heart tells me differently. By some sleight of mind I convince myself that, if things get difficult, all I need to do is hack a bigger hold in the snow with my ice axe or thrust my crampon points further into the ice. This is pure nonsense, of course, but that isn't the point. What is important for my ability to climb is my belief in it.

Nevertheless, the series of climbs that constituted our sole winter season on the Ben was to prove a salutary lesson for both Sandy and myself. I wish I could say we front-pointed up some startling new lines that had previously been considered unconscionable by the worthies of the Scottish Mountaineering Club. Alas, the reality was somewhat different. Even in gullies that some stalwarts used to *descend* from the summit plateau, we rarely managed to squirm our way up.

There was always a good reason for our failure. Sometimes the ice was too thin and brittle. Sometimes the snow was too deep and soft. Sometimes a gale threatened to peel us off the face of the mountain. Sometimes spindrift reduced visibility to zero. Yes, there was always a good reason.

Over the course of the season, we began to acquire a reputation for our exploits. I briefly relate a few incidents in *The Joy of Hillwalking*. There was the time, during one December retreat down South Castle Gully, when Sandy abseiled *through* the snow slope into a cave formed behind it by a rock overhang.

If Sandy had known he would have to jump down this...

On another occasion, we were actually within touching distance of the plateau, only to be stopped by a ginormous overhanging cornice that blocked the exit from our gully. The traditional method of tackling such an obstacle is to burrow through it, but a few hacks with an ice axe revealed it to be about as stable as blancmange and we retreated at pace.

Even more amusingly, we once ground to a halt on a snow step that provided a brief respite between two ice falls in a steep snow gully. The step was some three metres wide from one side of the gully to the other, and some four metres long from the lip of the ice fall below, which we had just climbed, to the foot of the ice fall above, which towered overhead.

I belayed securely to a rock projection while Sandy led the upper ice fall. Half an hour passed. He had progressed maybe six metres or so, and further progress was deemed impossible. I prepared to retreat without fuss. It was normal.

It was at this point that Sandy informed me he could neither climb back down nor find a secure belay from which to abseil. I had no time for such shilly-shallying. I was beginning to lose the feeling in my feet. 'Jump!' I yelled up to him. I shall not repeat what he yelled back. All he could see from his vantage point was a postage-stamp-sized landing spot beside me and, beyond, the lower ice fall disappearing into the abyss. If he managed not to break a leg on landing… and rolled with the impact…

'Jump!' I cried again. 'I have you.' He leaned out to look then retreated and hugged an ice bulge. 'Oh, man', I heard. He searched again for an abseil point, looked out again, dangled his foot over a scrape of ice… My fingers were becoming as numb as my toes, but I suffered in silence as best as I could. Had he no compassion?

In the end I nearly had to pull him down. With a great cry, he launched himself into space, cleared the ice fall and landed in a heap beside me. I yanked the slack rope taut as quick as I could, but it wasn't needed. The hollow made by his fall cushioned his landing, held him fast and stopped him rolling over the lower ice fall. The look he gave me is best described as old-fashioned. I shrugged. 'I told you it was fine.'

And that was that. While we still had warmth enough left in our hands for rope work, we used my belay point to abseil down the lower ice fall and glissade down to Coire Leis.

There was no debriefing, no questioning, no recrimination. It had been another good battle. Another exploit had been added to the canon. We sat cradling pints beside a log fire in a local hostelry and planned the next one.

28

Hooves from Hell

THERE'S NOTHING more disconcerting than things that go bump in the night. Fear of the unknown is hard-wired into the human brain from a time when we sat in caves and fretted about the creatures that were skulking out there in the darkness, waiting to get us. Even today, in certain parts of the world, there are stories of fabulous creatures that hide in the wilds, still waiting to get us. The Pacific coast of America has its Sasquatch or Bigfoot, Russia its Almasty and the Himalayas its Yeti. Many of us who live in cities struggle to find such tales any more believable than those of our own Loch Ness Monster. But we might be wrong.

Recent DNA testing of skin and hair purported to belong to such creatures has yielded surprising results. All Sasquatch and Almasty samples tested belonged to common mammals such as horse and raccoon, but some Yeti samples, from geographically diverse regions of the Himalayas, were more difficult to identify. The belonged to a polar bear. Not just any polar bear, but an ancient type of polar bear that existed before modern polar and other bears diverged into different species. Sightings reported by experienced mountaineers over the decades may not have been figments of the imagination after all. It appears that the Yeti may indeed exist.

The same can probably not be said for the nearest creature we have to a Yeti in the UK: the Big Grey of Ben Macdui. More than one experienced mountaineer has felt stalked by this monstrous apparition in swirling Cairngorm mist. Celebrated Victorian Alpinist Professor Norman Collie, not a man to be easily fooled, even fled the mountain to escape him.

It is in mist and darkness that sight fails and imagination takes over, summoning up ancient dreads. Mind you, there are still times when there really is something out there that can eat you.

Some environmentalists even regard this as a necessary condition of true wilderness. We're talking bears.

Be they black, grizzly or polar, bears are dangerous creatures that are best avoided. Unfortunately, they inhabit the kind of country that many of us like to visit, which makes hiking in such places potentially hazardous. Precautions to take include attaching a 'bear bell' to your pack, to warn of your presence, and cooking and storing smelly food a good distance away from a campsite. If precautions fail, strategies to deal with an encounter range from waving one's arms around to appear larger, to using pepper spray to fend off an attack.

For reassurance in bear country, I also strap to my pack a miniature teddy bear given to me by a concerned friend. The Bear With No Name is an ornery critter and he looks it. His nose is squashed and his nightshirt is torn. If there was any danger of underestimating his toughness you have only to look into his one remaining glass eye. This is one mean teddy. I convince myself that his big brothers won't want to mess with him.

I have yet to encounter a bear on my travels, but in bear country the possibility is never far from the mind. When sequestered within the confines of one's own private cave (i.e. tent), it is easy to read ursine significance into every outside sound, be it the snap of a twig, the sough of a breeze, the scampering of a squirrel or the crack of a falling pebble. Irrationally, annoyingly, it is all too easy to become a cowering caveman once again.

Those of us who have spent many nights in bear country have heard many unidentifiable wild animals outside the tent, and not all such close encounters need be traumatic. At 3,000m in the Rocky Mountains, I awoke one freezing morning to find myself spooning a large animal of some kind. I was in my sleeping bag, it was outside the tent, but it had snuggled into my body, presumably for warmth. It was the size and shape of a wolf or a mountain lion. When I gave a start, it ran off, making no sound from which I could infer its species.

Whatever it was, I felt an affinity with that creature. I may have brought my shelter and food with me rather than live off the land, but for the duration of my trip I was equally self-sufficient. In that vast, uncaring landscape, we were fellow living beings.

On the other hand, a wild camp on a high Pyrenean plateau resulted in one of the most terrifying experiences of my life. Philip and I were woken in the middle of the night by distant snorting sounds. They became louder. There was the clip-clop of hooves. Wild horses? They began to trot, then gallop. They were in full flight, hurtling towards us. The ground on which we lay shook with the thunder of their hooves. They would fail to see us in the black night. We would be trampled to death. We lay there unable to move, waiting for the inevitable.

The beasts came to an abrupt halt at the tent and snorted around its perimeter. We felt their breath billow the flysheet beside our heads. Then, just as abruptly, they were gone. We heard not a single neigh, just that awful, spectral snorting. We still only assume they were horses. For all we know, as we recall the primeval fear that gripped us when faced with the unseen onslaught, they were disembodied Hooves from Hell out to get us!

Pointless Pursuits

29

Ben Neverest

I'VE NEVER BEEN known to be willingly impartial to a silly adventure in the mountains.

Sir Hugh Munro failed to climb all but three of his famous list of Scottish 3,000ft mountains. In 1991, to celebrate the centenary of the first publication of Munro's Tables, Robin Campbell carried a life-size effigy of its author to the three summits for a 'posthumous' completion of his Munro round. I wish I'd thought of that.

29 May 2003, was the 50th anniversary of the first ascent of Mount Everest by Hillary and Tenzing, and it felt necessary to commemorate the occasion in some way. A repeat ascent was obviously out of the question, both practically and financially. I shall probably never have the ability or funds to climb the world's highest mountain now, but I console myself with the fantasy of being the oldest person ever to do so. Usefully, this is one ambition that can never be thwarted and to which I can cling until the day I die.

In 2003 the most appropriate substitute ascent Allan and I could come up with was the ascent of the highest mountain in our own country: Ben Nevis, renamed Ben Neverest for the day. Allan and I were imaginative souls. Glen Nevis was our base camp, the rock steps of the Mountain Track were our Khumbu Ice Fall, Lochan Meall an t-Suidhe half-way up was our South Col. A jaunt up the track would suffice for the ascent route as the important thing was not the journey but the destination.

The not-so-well-dressed hillwalker

Hillary and Tenzing had reached the summit at 11.30am. A quick internet search revealed that Nepal time was five and three-quarter hours ahead of GMT. For verisimilitude, we therefore had to be at the summit at 5.15pm. As it was a cold and drizzly day, we wouldn't want to hang around up there for too long, so we delayed setting off until the early afternoon. By that time, more than the usual number of weekday walkers were already coming down. We surmised that they too had been celebrating the occasion but had failed to go the extra mile and summit at the correct time, which enabled us to pass them with smug satisfaction.

The summit was deserted by the time we reached it. Having overestimated our ascent time and arrived an hour early, we took shelter in the observatory ruins from the cold north wind that raked the summit plateau. The hour passed slowly. As numbness crept into our bodies, conversation sagged and spirits along with it, but we weren't going to give up on a ridiculous enterprise just because it was becoming more ridiculous by the minute.

Finally, the appointed time arrived. To emphasise the surreal nature of the occasion, I had for some reason decided that, for commemorative photographs, I would change into beach shorts and Hawaiian shirt. This was a step too far for my companion, who merely grinned at me indulgently. I grinned back through chattering teeth as he took the photographs. When I changed back into more appropriate hill gear, my fingers were too numb to tighten laces. Even at a breakneck descent speed, it took some time to restore warmth.

It was only when we reached the glen that it dawned on me that my arithmetic skills had let me down. I had omitted to take British Summer Time into account. Nepal time was currently only four and three-quarter hours ahead. Our earlier smugness had been (not for the first time) entirely misplaced.

Worse was to follow. The next day I had another revelation about world time zones. If Nepal was four and three-quarter hours *ahead* of BST, we were four and three-quarter hours *behind* Nepal. In other words, we should have been at the summit of the Ben four and three-quarter hours *before* 11.30am, i.e. at 6.45am.

On receiving this update, Allan shrugged resignedly, accustomed by now to the unpredictable outcomes of those escapades of mine for which he signed up. I was unrepentant. I chose to view my perfectly understandable oversight in a more constructive light. What had begun as a pointless and surreal exercise had ended in even more pointless and surreal fashion. This was an even more welcome outcome, I decided. Serendipity. Would you care to see some photographs of a shivering beach bum grinning maniacally in a Hawaiian shirt at the top of Ben Nevis at precisely 5.15 BST on 29 May 2003?

30

The Tri-Country Day Hike

IN THE SAME way that I lack the gene to seek thrills (see *Seconds Away*), I can muster no desire to break records. The Three Peaks Challenge, the Bob Graham Round, bagging all the Munros in as little time as possible, climbing as many peaks as possible in 24 hours... not interested. Occasionally I challenge myself to better a personal best, but that's merely a random exercise in motivation. After all, if I want to set a new PB, I have only to climb a mountain I haven't climbed before.

As with many of the trips described in this book, it's more a sense of the ridiculous than driving ambition that underpins many of the odd projects with which I find myself involved. During a European road trip, for instance, it occurred to me that the close proximity of some national borders, together with favourable geography, might enable more than one country highpoint to be visited in a day.

The revelation came to me at the Drielandenpunt, the highest point in Holland. As the name implies, it is the meeting point of three countries: Holland, Belgium and Germany. Belgium's highpoint lay close to the roadside less than a couple of hours drive away. Germany's highpoint, the Zugspitze (2,962m), was a day's drive too far away in southern Germany but, just south of Belgium, Luxembourg's highpoint was again close to the roadside and surely within reach. I wasn't interested in breaking any record, as that would largely depend on driving speed between the three locations, but the opportunity of bagging three country highpoints in one day was too good to miss. Is there *anywhere* else in the world where this is possible?

Not surprisingly, the three easily reached summits are popular individual objectives in their own right. According to the peakbagger.com website, they are the fifth, sixth and ninth most

Climb the steps to bag Belgium's highpoint

ascended of all European country highpoints. Only Ben Nevis (UK), Mont Blanc (France), Zugspitze (Germany) and Carrantuohill (Ireland) are more popular, with Galdhøpiggen (Norway) and Teide (Tenerife, Spain) sneaking in at seventh and eighth.

The Drielandenpunt is a wooded hilltop, more correctly known as the Vaalserberg, in the southeast corner of Holland. Those who think that the country is flat should note the presence of a chairlift and Alpine slide just down the road. With a height of 322.7m, it is easily reached by a short walk (uphill, mind you!) from the car park. You can get higher and see over the trees by climbing a metal tower. There's also a maze where, embarrassingly for my navigational credentials, and despite several visits, I have yet to find my way out without assistance.

The Belgian highpoint, the Signal de Botrange (694m) is the highest part of a broad plateau known as the Hautes Fagnes (High Fens) and the road passes right over it. There's a café here and, beside it, a six-metres-high tower with steps that allow you to reach the giddy height of 700m. After the two-hour drive from the Dreilandenpunt, Wendy and I hiked from the car to the café and climbed the steps. The Signal itself is an adjacent communications tower, the top of which reaches the grand height of 718m.

Continuing southwards through rolling countryside, a fine motorway bridged valleys and cut through hills as it sped us down to northern Luxembourg. The country highpoint, called Bourgplatz (559m) in my guidebook, was virtually on the border. There was another tower and a roadside plaque that celebrated its exalted position. Again we hiked from the car to the plaque.

And that was that. Mission accomplished. Admittedly, it was an adventure that required more driving than walking, and not an exercise that required much… um… exercise. But we hiked to every highpoint, so it counted. More enjoyable walking awaited further down into Luxembourg, in the region known locally as Little Switzerland. Here, labyrinthine little valleys led deep into verdant greenwood, where metal ladders descended through canyon-like fissures in cavern-like darkness. But that's another story.

The trip I describe took place in the early 1990s. The date is important because in 1994 it was discovered that, in a field just along the road from Bourgplatz, there is a hilltop called Knieff that, at 560m, is one metre higher. So it seems that, should the opportunity present itself, I shall have to go back and do it all again. Which, in retrospect, simply makes the original endeavour all the more entertainingly ridiculous.

31

The King of all Ben Lomonds

THE 18TH AND 19TH centuries saw a great British diaspora to all parts of the globe, the consequence either of imperial ambition or of a desire simply to escape dire economic conditions back home. Destitute Scottish and Irish families especially undertook perilous sea journeys that saw many perish en route. Those who survived to make a life in strange new lands often discovered a new fondness for what they had left behind. When a rare shower passed over the Australian outback, Scottish settlers would leave their shack, stand in the rain and weep with nostalgia.

Like all immigrants, they sought to retain some reminder of their homeland. It's no surprise that there's an Edinburgh in Australia and a Glasgow in Suriname, and several instances of each in Canada and the USA. For Scots, the desire to give their surroundings a familiar name extended to mountains too. The English designated no Scafell Pike, the Welsh no Snowdon, the Irish no Carrantuohill, but Scottish emigrants took their two most popular peaks with them: Ben Nevis and Ben Lomond.

In Hong Kong, the most northerly 300m hill was appointed Ben Nevis (489m). It retained the name until 1997, when the Chinese took over administration of the region and renamed it Hung Fa Chai. There's still a Ben Nevis on Spitsbergen Island in the Arctic. With a height of 922m, it may just count as another Munro.

Ben Lomonds are more widespread. In various states of the USA, Ben Lomond is, among other things, a wine region, a school and more than one town. In Australia, it is the highest village in New South Wales. Its 1,370m elevation even makes it higher than the original Scottish peak. In Tasmania, Ben Lomond is a national park whose highpoint (Legges Tor, 572m) is the second highest summit on the Australian island.

There are also two mountains named after the Scottish original: one in New Zealand and one in the USA. Both are prominent peaks, named because their pyramid-shaped appearance is reminiscent of the original, with a long, gentle ridge on one side of the summit and a steeper drop on the other. Both also dominate lakes that rival Loch Lomond for picturesqueness: New Zealand's has its Lake Wakatipu and America's its Great Salt Lake.

All three Ben Lomonds are justly popular and have much to recommend them as hiking objectives. The original Ben Lomond (974m) stands proud above the shores of its famous loch, its

Utah's Ben Lomond

accessible position on the edge of the Highlands gives it great views in all directions, its renovated path gives a straightforward all-weather ascent, its craggy northern corrie makes it a spectacular winter mountain and its surrounding fleshpots make great refreshment stops after an ascent.

New Zealand's Ben Lomond (1,748m) stands on the outskirts of Queenstown on South Island and was named by the 19th-century Scottish settler, Duncan McAusland. A good trail climbs to the summit through pine forest, across moorland and up a steep, sometimes rocky ridge. The Skyline Gondola can be used to gain height and give a return summit trip of 5.6ml and c.950m of ascent.

America's Ben Lomond (2,960m) is the highest of the three, being three times as high as Scotland's. It was again named by Scottish settlers and, being just shy of 3,000m, is almost a metric Munro itself. Situated on the precipitous Wasatch Front, a chain of the Rocky Mountains, it soars over the Great Salt Lake and the town of North Ogden in northern Utah. Its eye-catching west face forms a craggy headwall familiar to all drivers speeding along the adjacent Interstate I-15.

It occurred to me, as a confirmed existentialist, that climbing all three Ben Lomonds would make a suitably pointless and entertaining exercise. As a UK-based hiker with limited resources, it was not a project into which I'd want to put a lot of time and money at the expense of other adventures, but it could remain a speculative goal in case the opportunity ever arose.

I have yet to explore New Zealand, but in 2013 Sandi and I found ourselves in Salt Lake City with a day to spare. As we watched Ben Lomond's western crags glow sunset red above the shimmering surface of the Great Salt Lake, deciding how to spend that day required little deliberation.

There are two main ascent routes. The short northern approach (three miles each way, 366m of ascent) was out of bounds as it required a four-wheel-drive vehicle to reach the trailhead. We had to settle for the lengthy southern approach, known as the North Skyline Trail (8.2ml each way, 1,100m of ascent), which at least had the advantage of following the scenic south ridge. It begins at a nick on the skyline of the Wasatch Front called the North Ogden Divide, where a paved road facilitates access.

The day of the ascent began with the summit in cloud, as though the mountain was determined to make us feel truly at home. A zigzagging trail climbed through forest, bush and luxuriant vegetation on the moister east side of the ridge. Halfway up, it crossed to the drier west side of the mountain, opening up infinite views westwards over the endless horizons of the Great Salt Lake.

At the foot of the final pyramid, steeper zigzags climbed 270m to the abrupt summit, where the cloud cleared just as we arrived. The vast view, and the prospect of a tiring return trip, made it a difficult spot to tear ourselves away from. On descent, the long miles in scorching afternoon sun began to tell, and the final zigzags down to the North Ogden Divide seemed to take forever.

From a mixture of exposure, exhilaration and exhaustion, we arrived back at the trailhead glowing as red as Lomond's evening crags. It had been a tough hike, but we would have expected no less from the King of All Ben Lomonds.

Now… two down, one to go.

32

Sand Mountaineering

IN THE AMERICAN southwest, a happy combination of geology and weather has resulted in the formation not only of canyons and buttes but also of sand mountains that rise to a height of 750ft (230m) above their base and beg to be climbed.

That amount of ascent may sound trivial when compared to the elevation gain of a typical day's hillwalking, yet sand mountaineering requires an inordinate amount of effort. Add to that a remote location, extreme heat and a wilderness environment, and it is no wonder that few people even attempt to reach the summits.

The Big Four sand mountains are found in Nevada, Colorado and California. Nevada's 600ft Sand Mountain is a *seif* dune ('seif' is Arabic for 'sword'), consisting of a single, snaking ridge that can be reached by a direct climb up one of the lateral walls. The other three are *barchans* (crescent-shaped dunes), or rather complex pyramids of barchans, one on top of another.

In Colorado's Great Sand Dunes, two miles of sustained dune work is required to reach the highest sand mountain in North America – the 750ft Star Dune. In California, Kelso Dunes reach a height of 600ft, while Eureka Dunes rise to 700ft on the fringes of Death Valley.

Great Sand Dunes is America's newest (2004) national park and is consequently the most popular of the Big Four sites but, for connoisseurs of sand mountaineering, Eureka Dunes brook no equal. They dominate the south end of the heat-blasted Eureka Valley, a great flat trench between the Last Chance Mountains and the Saline Range, which close in to trap the wind-blown sand. The nearest aid is 50 miles away, so this is no place to run out of gas or succumb to heatstroke.

The compactness of the 700ft sand mountain that forms the

highpoint of the dunes gives it very steep slopes. This adds to its aesthetic appeal and makes it seem much higher than altitude measurements estimate it to be. It covers an area of only four square miles, but you can pack an awful lot of complexity into four square miles.

Viewed from the bottom, the three-dimensional maze of barchans rises to a distant sky-touching summit shimmering in the heat haze. Once into that maze, the clean geometric lines and planes formed by the ridges and faces of the barchans take on the mesmerising appearance of a Cubist masterpiece. Changing patterns of light and shade further add to the feeling of other-worldliness. Never did sand exhibit so many different golden hues, never did shadow contain so many shades of black, never did sky appear so richly blue.

All this made the route to the summit razorback (knife-edge ridge) surprisingly difficult to fathom. Sandi and I made good progress across the gentle lower barchans, but increasingly steep slopes, known as slipfaces, soon threatened to stop us in our tracks completely. The sand had the consistency of bottomless soft snow. Wind whipped it into whirlwind-like 'sand devils' that made keeping to our chosen line impossible. Sometimes the whole mountain seemed to shift beneath our feet, adding an extra layer of surrealness to the experience.

Every upward step disintegrated as soon as weight was transferred to it, making it necessary to leap rapidly upwards with the other foot to prevent all height gain being lost. Only by repeating this process *ad infinitum* was it possible to make any progress at all, in short, sharp, energy-sapping bursts that left our throats parched from hyperventilating in 50°C heat.

It was impossible to maintain any rhythm or even an upright posture. Regular time-outs were necessary to empty trainers overflowing with uncomfortable sand. In places, the only way to move onwards and upwards was to thrust fists into the sand for added purchase and climb on all fours. With sand temperatures of 60°C scorching our hands, this made the whole adventure even more radical.

Kelso Dunes summit ridge

Meanwhile, directly above us, so near yet so far, suspended on the skyline against that infinite blue sky, the summit razorback hung like a giant wave frozen in the breaking. Frozen? If only.

At one point, stranded on a particularly vertiginous slipface where every upward step simply deposited us back in the same place, the only possibility of further progress lay in a sideways, crablike traverse to the right-hand edge, in the hope of finding less steep ground beyond. By such zigzagging tactics, to say nothing of a determination that only hillwalkers intent on a summit would understand, we at last managed to reach the skyline… only to find that the actual highpoint lay a further couple of hundred metres away along the undulating summit ridge.

In the extreme heat, with diminishing water supplies (we had grossly underestimated the amount required), it was important now not to be drawn onwards beyond our physical limits. On the return trip those undulations would have to be negotiated again before a sand glissade down to the valley.

If the ground had been stable, the dips in the ridge would

have seemed minimal, but the soft sand turned them into major obstacles, on a razorback that was as sharp as they come. The knife-edge crest demanded a technique akin to tightrope walking. As it disintegrated beneath our feet at every step, tumbles were unavoidable. As for the ascents out of the dips, minor though they were, they could be accomplished only by a pioneering climbing technique we developed and which I can only describe as *rush-and-flail*.

Was the effort worth it? You bet it was! Standing atop the furnace-like summit of Eureka Dunes Sand Mountain, with 360° of shimmering wilderness veiling infinite horizons all around, was one of those supreme moments out of time.

33

Brollibond or Bust

WE'VE ALL SEEN those grainy pictures of Mallory, Irvine and other early 20th-century stalwarts, toiling gallantly up Everest in their tweeds. Tweeds?! It beggars belief. These days, many of us wouldn't venture to the corner shop in a slight drizzle without donning a Gore-Tex shell.

In the 1960s, when I began serious all-weather hillwalking, tweed knee-length breeches were still commonplace and Gore-Tex was a dream. Who would have believed that it was possible to manufacture a fabric that was both waterproof and breathable *at the same time*? Even Einstein would have rejected such a notion as being outwith the laws of physics.

Gore-Tex didn't appear on the market until 1978, SympaTex until 1986. The state of the art in upper body wear in the 1960s was the nylon cagoule. The very word *cagoule* summoned up images of an enervating battle against the elements on some Alpine north face. It was as though the mere purchase of a garment sporting such an exotic name would overnight confer on the wearer the skills of a Swiss guide.

The particular cagoule I set my heart on was a cool black and was long enough to double as a burka. It was purported to be waterproof, so it was fortunate for the makers that the Trades Description Act did not come into force until 1968. On its first outing in a typical Highland downpour, it performed admirably. On its second outing, it developed a slight dampness on the inside. On subsequent outings it leaked like a sieve at the merest threat of an overcast sky, sucking moist air from the atmosphere like a desert lungfish after years of drought.

Attempts to re-proof the garment by applying various (pre-Nikwax) water-repellent solutions proved fruitless. Despite this, I had no option but to persevere with it, as I could not afford a replacement. This at least improved fitness levels, as the only way to combat wind chill when wet was to keep moving.

For warmth, the latest *haute couture* offering was the *duvet*. The name now refers to a bed quilt, but in those days it applied to a bulky, down-filled jacket. Only Robin could afford one, and he made sure we knew it by wearing it everywhere, especially to the pub. The only place it was never seen was on the hill, because the volume of water it could assimilate would have made the Borg envious and was a lesson to all sponges. It may have been an ideal garment for the Alps or Himalayas, but something a tad more robust is required for even a brief Highland smirr.

I thought I'd discovered the answer on a trip to the Pyrenees. The local hikers wore cheap plastic ponchos that reached down to the knee and covered both the head and the rucksack. Why had no one thought of this before? Once you were ensconced inside, the sensation was one of wearing a mobile tent. The garment held little warmth but was completely windproof and waterproof, and its looseness allowed sufficient air circulation to prevent clamminess.

Back in the UK, my hill companions were dubious. I wore my new poncho only once. On a dreich day the Cairngorms, horizontal rain forced its way inside *from below* and wind turned it into a parasail. My companions were suitably and quite rightly smug.

The solution to our problems appeared to come in 1972. Its arrival was heralded by a photograph in a magazine of Don Whillans, no less, lying in 'the glacial waters of Patagonia' with a big grin on his face. He was wearing an oversuit made from a new kind of material called Brollibond. If it was good enough for Don, who had made the first ascent of the south face of K2, it could surely handle anything the Scottish winter could throw at us.

The lightweight blue fabric featured a polyurethane membrane that was completely waterproof and windproof. This was sandwiched between thin layers of warming foam, which were themselves sandwiched between thin layers of facing material. Unable to afford any of the manufactured garments, I bought four metres of the stuff and a pattern for trousers. I had never made any clothing before, but I had a university degree in psychology. How hard could it be?

I managed to fashion two legs, in the manner of cowboy chaps, and linked them together with a length of red tent repair tape. This ran under the crotch from the front of the waist to the back and resulted in a less than stylish item of apparel. It was also a less than successful item of hillwalking gear, as I had no means of adequately sealing the seams. A matching anorak, the result of over-vaunted ambition, remained a permanent work in progress. There was unexpectedly more skill to this tailoring lark than a psychology degree had prepared me for.

When used properly, Brollibond was indeed windproof and waterproof, but it lacked breathability. Rain collected in the outer layer of foam and perspiration in the inner, making the outside feel cold and the inside feel clammy. As usual, I persevered with my bespoke creations beyond the point of reason, until companions became embarrassed by my increasingly maverick appearance and threatened to boycott me.

In any event, Brollibond was soon to be consigned to history. Bob Gore discovered that stretching polytetrafluoroethylene

(PTFE) produced a microporous structure that allowed water vapour (perspiration) to pass through while remaining impervious to water droplets (rain). It was a eureka moment.

Tweed, nylon, Brollibond, microporous membrane... Has the evolution of outdoor clothing reached its zenith? Watch this space.

34

Highpointers and Peakbaggers

WHEN WE CLIMB a mountain, most of us want to reach the summit, and there's some special satisfaction to be had from reaching the *highest* summit. That's what makes Scafell Pike, Snowdon, Ben Nevis and Mount Everest more popular than surrounding summits of almost equal height.

But what next? How to choose what else to climb? Of course, every hill or mountain should be climbed for its own merit but, other things being equal, higher hills are always going to have a greater appeal than lower ones. It's the nature of the game... the Great Game, as it was known to Victorian Alpinists. That's where the climbing strategies known in the USA as highpointing and peakbagging come in.

Highpointing involves climbing the highpoints (i.e. the highest points) in a designated group: countries, regions, counties, national parks, islands, grid squares on an OS map... Bagging the highpoints of historic British counties, for instance, involves 95 trips. There are 48 county highpoints in England (including London), 14 in Wales and 33 in Scotland, although not all require as much effort as Ben Nevis. Excluding London (highpoint: High Holborn, 22m), the lowest highpoints of the three countries are Beacon Hill (103m) in Norfolk, Pantylladron (137m) in Glamorganshire and Cairnpapple Hill (312m) in West Lothian.

If, as a good European, you wish to bag the highpoints of the countries of the European Union, there are currently 28, of which France's Mont Blanc (4,810m) is the highest and Denmark's Møllehøj (171m) the lowest. Bagging the highpoints of the USA's 50 states is an even more awkward proposition. The highest is the redoubtable Mount McKinley (6,168m) in Alaska, while the lowest, not unexpectedly, is Florida's Britton Hill (105m). Delaware's highpoint is a marker on a street pavement. There's a slight hill below it and some sticklers for authenticity park at the bottom, put their boots on and walk up. Keen peakbaggers can join the Highpointers Club.

The ultimate highpointing challenge is the Seven Summits, comprising the highpoints of the 'seven continents' of the world: Aconcagua, McKinley, Mont Blanc, Elbrus, Everest, Kilimanjaro, Puncak Jaya and Kosciuszko. Bagging that septet requires not only dedication but also unlimited time and money. Nevertheless, it has been completed so many times (currently c.300) that in 2012 the even harder Seven Second Summits, e.g. replacing Everest with K2, was completed for the first time.

By its very nature, highpointing involves a good deal of travel, and this is one of the reasons why its close cousin peakbagging has become more popular in hillwalking circles. Peakbagging involves climbing all summits that reach a specified height in a range or country. The standout example in the UK is Munro bagging.

When Sir Hugh Munro, the third President of the Scottish Mountaineering Club, published his 'Tables of Heights over 3,000 Feet' in the 1891 edition of the SMC Journal, he could never have imagined the impact his list would have a century later. Choosing the criterion of 3,000ft (914m) in the imperial system of measurement as his cut-off point, he counted 283 separate Scottish mountains, now named Munros after him. Following additions and deletions over decades of re-measurement, currently by GPS satellite, the list currently contains 282.

It could have been so different. The Tables grew out of Victorian debates about entrance qualifications to the fledgling SMC, with heights such as 3,500ft also being considered. A cut-off point of 3,500ft (1,067m) would give 70 mountains, while 4,000ft (1,220m) would give only eight. A more modern metric cut-off point of 1,000m (3,280ft), giving 137 'metric Munros', has never captured the hillgoing public's imagination.

A list such as Munro's begs the question: when is a mountain a mountain? How far away and/or how deep must the intervening gap be for a second summit to count as a separate mountain rather than just a subsidiary top of the first one? Munro listed a further 255 'Tops' that were insufficiently separated to be recognised as different mountains themselves. Many Munroists bag these too.

The SMC also maintains a list of Furths, i.e. 3,000ft summits in the furth (rest of) the British Isles: 13 in Ireland, six in England and 15 in Wales. But are there really 15 in Wales? Does the bump of Carnedd Gwenllian count? Does the rock outcrop of Castell y Gwynt count? Such issues bedevil all lists. Also in Wales, the metric Munro concept has gained greater credence in recent years owing to the discovery (following re-measurement in 2010) that Glyder Fawr is 1.8m higher than was previously thought. It is now listed as 1,000.8m. This has upped the Welsh metric Munro total from four to five and played havoc with the well-established Welsh 1,000m Peaks Race.

Both highpointing and peakbagging have their adherents and their detractors. On the plus side, a well-chosen list can give you a lifetime's exercise. On the minus side, you may be lured by the heightism inherent in such a project into ignoring some interesting hills that fall below the magic height, e.g. the 884m non-Munro of The Cobbler in Argyll.

At best, there's something endearingly eccentric about the whole enterprise. At worst, it's the hillwalking equivalent of trainspotting. And, please, spare me yet another self-congratulatory book relating yet another marathon ticking expedition by someone who has climbed all the Munros in summer, in winter, running, hopping, blindfolded, on hands and knees, backwards...

Munro's list was such a success that it spawned countless more. The 1921 edition of Munro's Tables also included J. Rooke

Corbett's list of Highland mountains with heights between 2,500ft and 2,999ft ('Corbetts'), and Percy Donald's list of hills in the Scottish Lowlands of 2,000ft or over ('Donalds'). Even today, the number of lists continues to grow. Take your pick from the following (incomplete) selection.

Grahams are the 223 Scottish hills between 2,000ft (609m) and 2,499ft (762m) with a prominence criterion (i.e. drop all around) of 150m (492ft). Murdos are the 443 Scottish mountains over 3,000ft with a prominence criterion of 30m (98ft). Marilyns are the 1,554 British mountains with a prominence criterion of 150m (492ft), regardless of height. Hewitts are the 528 British hills over 2,000ft with a prominence criterion of 30m. And so on.

Outside the UK, peakbaggers are routinely required to climb higher to attain their goal. At the next level up from Munros are the Cairngorms-like Catskills of New York State. The highest Catskill is 1,270mft Slide Mountain and the Catskill equivalent of Munro bagging is climbing the 35 mountains over 3,500ft (1,067m) high. It's not quite as simple as that, though. To join the Catskill 3,500 Club, you not only have to climb them all in summer conditions, but also four of them again (including Slide) in winter conditions.

Close by, and up another level, are the Adirondacks, which reach 1,629m at Mount Marcy. The equivalent to Munro bagging here is climbing all 48 peaks on the list of peaks over 4,000ft high. This list is as idiosyncratic as Munro's Tables. Owing to re-measurement, there are currently only 44 peaks over 4,000ft and, to confound the issue even further, climbing the 48 on the list entitles you to membership of the Adirondack Forty-Sixers.

This peculiar state of affairs has arisen because there were 46 qualifying peaks in 1918, when the list was first drawn up. Subsequent re-measurement has demoted four but raised another two to the magic figure, so now you are expected to climb 48.

Moving up another level, we reach the 3,000m peaks of the Pyrenees and the 4,000m peaks of the Alps. The precise number depends on the prominence criterion used. There are generally regarded to be 212 Pyrenean 3,000ers and 82 Alpine 4,000ers.

However, if a prominence criterion of 100m is applied, the Alpine list is reduced to 52. If a prominence criterion of 500m is applied, the list is reduced to 22.

The American equivalent of Alpine 4,000'ers is fourteeners, which are summits over 14,000ft (4,267m) high. Unlike their glaciated Alpine counterparts, most of these are accessible to walkers, including the highest outside Alaska: California's Mount Whitney (14,505ft/4,421m). The fourteener hotspot is Colorado, which has 54 of them, far more than any other state. Despite high altitude and occasional technical difficulty, bagging all 54 is a popular leisure activity.

Moving up more levels, we reach the peakbagger's earthly limits. Give or take a few, there are approximately 860 5,000m summits in the Andes, of which 102 are 6,000ers. Good luck with those. In the Himalayas, enumeration is even more difficult and estimates differ widely. One source gives 184 summits above 6,000m, of which 107 are above 7,000m, of which 14 are above 8,000m. Whatever the precise number, there should be more than enough to occupy inveterate peakbaggers with an enviable amount of time and money on their hands. Although... more than 30 of them have already scaled all 14 8,000'ers.

Unfortunately, their number will never include me. Oh well. Back in the real world, I still have more than enough ticks to add to more than enough lists to keep me more than happily occupied for more than one lifetime.

35

The Lost Art of Festering

IF YOU LOOK up the meaning of the verb 'to fester' in most dictionaries, you'll find only negative connotations concerning putrefaction, discharge and general all-round debilitation. Only a trusty dictionary will give you the more informal definition of 'to be inactive', and it is in this sense that the activity has a long and distinguished history in the annals of mountaineering.

Activity? Indeed. Festering involves prolonged confinement in a tent. It raises the pursuit of inactivity to such a high art form that it requires as much planning, dedication and perseverance as any more aerobic athletic endeavour. N.B. I admit to a personal interest here as it is the only aspect of mountaineering in which my ability matches my aspiration.

The ability to fester is a greatly under-appreciated outdoor skill. It's all very well romping around the hills, but you can't do that *all* the time. Every body needs a spot of rest and recuperation. Even on a week's holiday, with permanently beckoning peaks shimmering in constant heat haze, you're going to need a break at some point. And if you're camping in a remote location, what are you going to do but fester?

When it comes to matters of hillwalking prowess and climbing technique, I am the first to acknowledge my betters, but when it comes to festering I bow only to Sandy, my Ben Nevis ice-climbing leader. Sandy could fester for Britain. Several attempts to out-fester him, by myself and others, have all ended in failure. When we finally give up and answer the call of the hills once more, he emerges from his tent even more bedraggled than usual but grinning smugly. He knows he is the undisputed champion. Nonetheless, my own festering expertise is exceeded only by my falling expertise, and it is with no feigned humility that I offer some advice to neophytes.

A basic prerequisite for a successful fester, as in all fields of mountaineering, is good equipment. To survive for any length of time in a tent under normal British meteorological conditions, this begins with a good sleeping bag. Breaking the fester, in order to get up and move around to keep warm, is a beginner's mistake. By definition, a fester must avoid exercise at all costs. Eating, drinking and evacuating are permitted, but only when absolutely necessary.

There are, of course, rare climatic conjunctions when the

temperature rises and a sleeping bag is surplus to requirements. It may surprise beginners to learn that, on such occasions, a hot-day fester can be even more difficult to sustain than a cold-day fester. Staying cooped up in the heated interior of a tent, in a form of hibernation known as estivation, requires considerable stamina.

With regard to re-provisioning, a prolonged fester is more readily maintained if all food required is at hand. Cooking is best avoided, especially if safety concerns demand that it be undertaken in the forbidden zone, i.e. outside the tent. Rainwear, compass, first aid kit and similar hill gear should not be required if the fester is prepared correctly.

A common reason for fester failure is the urging of *al fresco* companions to undertake activity. Such exhortations can be especially awkward to refute if you are the driver of their sole means of transport to the pub. In such circumstances, it can be useful to have a good excuse for lassitude. Here are some suggestions. It can always be too hot or too cold. If not, you can feign recollection of one weather forecast that says it soon will be. Handy ailments that are easily faked include headache, stomach ache, muscle ache... in fact, any kind of ache.

You may think that doing nothing is easy, but prolonged inactivity is inimical to the human condition. It requires great dedication to achieve its purest form: free festering. This precludes the use of artificial aids such as playing cards, reading material or (even worse) wi-fi connection. It is the ultimate goal of the art form and something to which beginners should aspire.

I have free-festered in tents in all weathers, both at home and abroad. Third place in my Top Ten Festers goes to a camp in the Llanberis Pass in Snowdonia, in the days when camping was permitted there. With heavy rain and gale-force wind deterring even a cautious peek outside, there was minimal incentive even to jump in the car and head down to the pub. The more the flysheet whipped and flapped, the more I drew my sleeping bag around me, a cocoon of comfort against the ravages of the elements. The 24-hour fester, from evening to evening, was

Advanced festering

finally broken by a lessening on the Beaufort Scale and the lure of alcohol.

Runner-up spot goes to a fester at the head of a high valley in the Ubaye region of the French Alps. After a hot day's hike up the 3,340m Bric de Rubren, exhaustion and overcast skies made Jo and I loath to leave the tent. Our 30-hour fester was broken only by a need to replenish food stocks and a unique opportunity that was impossible to refuse. The nearest village was across the border in Italy. How many times in life do you get to shop for groceries in a different country?

We had to cross a high pass, descend to the village and re-ascend to our wilderness camp (a tad more slowly), laden with goodies. It was worth it. I can still taste that evening spread of fresh local produce, to say nothing of the single *bière* that was enough to knock us out.

Coming in at Number One on my list of Top Ten Festers is a two-day fester-thon in Glen Brittle on the Isle of Skye. To accomplished festerers, the location will come as no surprise. No mountains take so much out of you as the Cuillin in a heat wave. After several days of being cooked by solar rays bouncing around the rock cirques, the body is almost demanding respite, making conditions ideal for a prolonged fester.

This particular session was extended beyond the point of justifiability by a desire to out-fester Sandy, who had taken up residence in an adjacent tent. Of course it was an unwinnable contest. Even when I emerged squinting into the blinding sunlight, hungry and stiff, no sound emanated from his tent until I prevailed on him to poke his head out the flysheet. I can still see his creased features, the manic grin wider than ever.

In a world in which speed is such a prized commodity, be it for a road trip, for internet connectivity or simply for kicks, there is no doubt that the standard of festering has declined. More's the pity. Festering has so much to offer. Margaret Thatcher split opinion, but she was right when she said that one of the problems of the modern world is that too many people *feel* and not enough people *think*.

This point was illustrated by a recent study at the University of Virginia, which showed that even spending six to 15 minutes alone in a room with nothing to do but think was too much for most people. Some even preferred to administer electric shocks to themselves rather than be left alone with their thoughts.

If the human race is truly losing its ability for stillness and quiet – an evolutionary development hastened by the advent of mobile phones and social media – it is time to redress the balance. Let there be time for us to think. Let there be time for contemplation and for the inactivity that allows it to flourish. Let us go to the mountains and, when we get there, let us sometimes do nothing at all. Let us, in Walt Whitman's words, be 'both in and out of the game, watching and wondering at it'.

Devil's Advocate

36

Blowing Hot and Cold

AN APOLOGETIC television weather forecaster once informed his viewers that 'there won't be a lot of weather tomorrow'. At least that was a welcome change from the usual biased judgements that pass for meteorological reportage, and not just on television and radio. When it comes to weather, the entire British media displays a prejudice that would be unacceptable in any other field. Here are two recent tabloid headlines: 'Nightmare of winter begins' and 'Snow brings fresh misery'.

It's always the British winter that bears the brunt of the diatribe, couched in language replete with pejorative terminology. The country is *battered* by wind and *crippled* by snow. We're subjected to *blasts* of Arctic/Siberian weather and *cold snaps*, although it is never clear what exactly is going to snap. At least when it's *bone-chilling*, you know where you stand, even if it would be news to anatomists that bones can actually sense temperature. If the cold snap lasts, we may even find ourselves in a *deep freeze*. Has there ever been a *shallow* freeze?

Sometimes, parts of the country are *paralysed* or, even worse, *cut off*. But cut off from what? Oddly, London, where most of this guff is written, never seems to be cut off. At the first sign of a gently falling snowflake, the authorities may even deliberately sever some lines of communication by closing snow gates on roads. No doubt that first snowflake is a harbinger of the inevitable *heavy* snowfall that will render road conditions *nightmarish*. What nightmares they must have in Canada and Scandinavia.

All winter weather is vilified in this manner as *bad*. Naughty, naughty weather. What gives the media the right to impose such moral judgements? Why is winter to be endured rather than enjoyed? As children, before we have it drummed into us by the incessant anti-winter propaganda, we love snow.

Summer is never demonised in such disparaging terms. We may have a bone-chilling winter, but we never have a bone-melting summer, even though it is heat, not cold, that is the more difficult condition for human beings to counter. If it's cold you can wear more clothing, but when it's hot there's a limit to what you can remove.

We're never *blasted* by the sun's rays, although they are more dangerous to us than any winter weather phenomenon. Such is our misplaced admiration for solar radiation that we even deliberately seek it out to damage our skin. Tanning is nothing more than an adaptation to that damage, caused by the increased secretion of melanin into skin cells to combat an excess of ultraviolet light. Curiously, we are conditioned to find that attractive. No one wants their skin to look like leather, but what is leather if not tanned skin?

Anything other than sunshine is reported in deprecatory terms, even rain. Rain is essential to our ecology and economy, yet it gets the same bad press as all other forms of precipitation. No wonder, as Richard Burton noted in his recently published private records, it makes Brits 'pinched and puny and mean'. Maybe I'm fortunate – I can afford clothes and, in any case, my skin happens to be waterproof.

Weather systems that bring dry weather are routinely referred to as 'highs' rather than anticyclones. Those that bring unsettled weather are referred to as 'lows' rather than cyclones. Using such emotive terms to describe the phenomena by relative air pressure rather than by direction of wind circulation is typical of media negativity. The words are even daubed all over weather charts to reinforce their emotive power. In case we still don't get the picture, lows are further described as depressions. Who could ever find any cheer in a depression?

It's time we reclaimed our British weather from these naysayers. In some deserts it hardly ever rains; in some rainforests it hardly ever stops. On the equator it gets dark at the same time every day; dusk as we know it does not exist. In some parts of the Andes it is almost perpetual springtime. How boring.

We are lucky to inhabit an island that has such a wonderfully varied temperate climate. Meteorologists, of all people, should realise this and reflect our good fortune in their bulletins.

37

Leave No Trace

HIDDEN AWAY IN the remote Needles district of Utah's Canyonlands National Park, far from any road, is a deep, vertical-walled ravine called The Joint. In the heart of The Joint, accessible only to those hardy souls who make the punishing approach trek across the sun-blasted expanse of Chesler Park, the narrows open up into a grotto-like space that sun and wind never reach. Here is to be found one of the most unexpected and riveting displays of man-made rock architecture on earth.

Hundreds of cairns dot the uneven ground, but they are no lumpen, hastily cobbled together stone pyramids. Unlike the cairns we see on British hills, these are ethereal constructions that lean and teeter at unlikely angles in gravity-defying fashion. In the ever-still air, large rocks balance precariously on pebbles, stones overlap stones by the sheerest edge, flimsy rock lattices form intricate wall-like structures, and zigzagging edifices rise in implausible fashion, each arm so perfectly counterbalanced that the merest breeze would demolish the whole.

This hidden art installation, fashioned by passing canyoneers taking time out in the cool shade, constitutes nothing less than a beautiful, three-dimensional, Pointillist landscape. Like all good art, it has that elusive 'wow' factor missing from so many modern artistic conceptualisations. It puts Turner Prize endeavours to shame.

If only the same could be said for British cairn construction attempts. Take our highest mountain. The summit plateau of Ben Nevis is a prime example of a *felsenmeer* or *blockfield*, a patchwork of broken rocks formed by a series of freeze-thaw cycles during the last Ice Age. There is plenty of material here to build cairns, and every passing tourist seems to want to leave his or her mark by lumping a few rocks together into a misshapen heap. The 'Kilroy wuz here' syndrome. No rockscape could be in greater contrast to The Joint.

In the late 20th century, as the Ben's popularity exploded, the summit cairns became an increasing eyesore and a navigational danger. In foul weather they could be mistaken for route markers and lead people astray. Add a growing number of personal memorials of various kinds and the summit plateau was beginning to look like a cross between a brickyard and a cemetery.

The desire to commemorate the lives of loved ones is understandable but, as more people and pets die, there has to be a limit to how many memorials one location can support. The scattering of ashes on mountaintops has already got out of hand. Phosphates and other minerals from cremated bones stimulate plant growth and alter mountain ecosystems to such an extent that the Mountaineering Council of Scotland has appealed for people to desist from the practice. Football clubs have similarly had to stop the scattering of fans' ashes on their grounds to preserve pitches. When the John Muir Trust purchased Ben Nevis in 2000, they had the good sense to remove the cairns, the memorials and tons of litter in an attempt to restore the summit to a more natural state.

Some mountains have fared even worse than the Ben, with officially sanctioned larger memorials defacing their summits. The one that causes the greatest visual pollution in Scotland is a large iron cross on the southeast shoulder of Ben Ledi near Callander. In the Catholic countries of the European Alps, such crosses routinely disfigure many mountaintops. On a cloud-whipped Austrian peak, I was once struck by lightning attracted by one of the iron monstrosities.

An even more execrable blot on the Austrian landscape is the sculptor Anthony Gormley's so-called Horizon Field, an outland-ish vanity project that consists of 100 naked life-size figures of himself placed on mountainsides above 2,000m. However justified by specious artistic reasons, this is intrusive vandalism on the grand scale. Do *you* want your Alpine view marred by a naked sculptor?

Other sad people find that the only way they can think of to leave their mark on society is to carve their names into tree trunks, or arrange loose rocks to spell their name on the ground. One prime location scarred by the latter activity is Arthur's Seat, the 251m landmark in the centre of Edinburgh. Of course, none of the vandals who commit these puerile acts care about nature. With the ever-increasing popularity of outdoor activities, and the corresponding abuse of the countryside, this makes it ever more important to educate them in minimal environmental impact.

In the USA in the 1990s, the National Parks Service, the Forest Service and other organisations developed the Leave No Trace programme for this very purpose. The programme encourages people to follow seven principles:

1   Plan Ahead and Prepare.
2   Travel and Camp on Durable Surfaces.
3   Dispose of Waste Properly.
4   Leave What You Find.
5   Minimise Campfire Impacts.
6   Respect Wildlife.
7   Be Considerate of Other Visitors.

A Center for Outdoor Ethics was established in Boulder, Colorado, and this now has international branches around the world. Ireland joined in 2006. At the time of writing, the centre has established partnerships in the UK with organisations and companies such as the Wilderness Foundation and Wildtrek, but the country as a whole still lacks a coordinated national effort. Every year the JMT still has to remove tons of rubbish from Ben Nevis. The need for Leave No Trace has never been greater. Check it out at http://lnt.org.

38

A Mountain by Any Other Name

A MOUNTAIN'S NAME can add much to its allure. Who would not want to pit one's wits against The Executioner on Skye, stand at the seemingly scrumptious summit of Yorkshire's Roseberry Topping or see how flat the summit of South Africa's Table Mountain really is?

The simple appellation Mont Blanc (White Mountain) perfectly suits the snow dome that is the highest mountain in Western Europe. What more solid name could there be for a Big Mountain in Scotland than Gaelic's sturdy Ben More? What a tale could be woven around the Swiss triumvirate of the Eiger, the Jungfrau and the Mönch (the Ogre, the Maiden and the Monk).

Scotland too has its Maiden (A' Mhaighdean) as well as a Sugar Loaf (Suilven), a Forge (An Teallach), a Devil's Point and even the enchanting Hill of the Round Corrie of Little Blisters (Braigh Coire Chruin-bhalgain). The island of Rum has a clutch of fine old Norse mountain names such as Askival, Hallival and Trallval. England has its imaginatively-named Saddleback, Wales its very own Matterhorn, which goes by the appropriately abrupt appellation Cnicht. The names of British mountain and hill ranges are equally enticing. England has its Malverns and Mendips, Wales its Glyders and Rhinogs, Scotland its Mamores and Cuillin.

The names are of mostly ancient origin. Most great mountain names are. In olden times, no one would have named a summit Sgurr Julius Caesar, Mount Ethelred the Unready or Pik Ivan the Terrible. Not so these days. Personal names are invading our mountains.

The most climbed 7,000m peak in the world stands in the Pamirs on the border of Tajikistan and Kyrgyzstan. It was originally named Mount Kaufman for the first governor of Turkestan. During the years of the Soviet Union it was renamed Pik Lenin. Not even Russians want to climb that today. Tajikistan now calls it Abu Ali Ibn Sino, while Kyrgyzstan calls it Pik Sary Tash. The highest peak in Tajikistan was named Pik Stalin when it was discovered in 1933. It became Pik Communism in 1962 and is now named Pik Ismoil Somoni for the ruler of an ancient Persian dynasty.

By all means name a New York airport for American President J. F. Kennedy, but not the highest unclimbed peak in North America. That fate befell a 4,000m mountain in Canada in 1965. In the USA itself, presidential names are commonplace: Mount Adams, Mount Roosevelt, Mount Woodrow Wilson... Many states have a Mount Lincoln. Colorado has two. The highest mountain in New Hampshire is Mount Washington. Vermont even has a Presidential Range with no fewer than 12 peaks named for former presidents.

There is as yet no Mount Nixon, and this exemplifies one of the main problems with this approach to nomenclature. Whereas mountains are eternal (as good as, compared to our own time span), political worthiness is both ephemeral and disputable.

Castle Mountain in Alberta was renamed Mount Eisenhower following World War Two, but after growing objections it reverted to its original (and more imaginative) name in 1979. Alaska's Mount McKinley, the highest mountain in North America, was named in the 19th century for the 25th US president and is still

Phoenix's Squaw Peak... or is it Piestewa Peak?

known as such by the US Board of Geographical Names. The Alaska Board of Geographical Names, on the other hand, calls it Denali, its original name in the Athabaskan language. Attempts to have Denali replace McKinley nationwide have been blocked by the former President's home state of Ohio. At the time of writing, a proposal to change the name of Nevada's Frenchman Mountain to Mount Reagan is causing similar political waves.

It's not just politicians that are the subject of misplaced memorialism. Mount Whitney in the Sierra Nevada was named for the head of the California Geological Survey. The same range has an Evolution Basin whose surrounding mountains are named for pioneers of evolution theory such as Darwin, Spencer and Huxley.

In Phoenix, Arizona, Squaw Peak (named for the Algonquian term for a woman) was renamed Piestewa Peak in 2008 to honour a soldier killed in Iraq. And what are we to make of Utah's Mollie's Nipple, said to have been named for a rancher's wife?

The USA is the main but not the only culprit. Kyrgyzstan has a Pik Boris Yeltsin, a Pik Vladimir Putin and even a Pik Santa Claus. The highest mountains in Columbia are Mount Simon

Bolivar and Mount Cristobal Colon (Christopher Columbus). Mount Vinson, the highest peak in Antarctic, is named for the US Congressman who supported Antarctic research.

The issue is not one of worthiness but of whether mountain tops are the right place to honour *anyone*. If needs must, there are other ways of showing love and respect in the wilds. California's John Muir Trail honours the pioneer of conservation. The Scottish Mountaineering Club Hut on Ben Nevis commemorates Charles Inglis Clark, a club member who was killed in World War One. The Abruzzi Spur on K2 celebrates a 1909 expedition led by the Duke of the Abruzzi.

One of the reasons we go to the hills is 'to get away from it all', and the modern trend to fill the wilderness with reminders of what we're trying to get away from is as reprehensible as leaving litter and building personal or religious memorials. The most meaningful and beautiful names generally derive from to a time when our forebears were more in touch with the land. They used their imaginations to name mountains for colours, shapes, flora, fauna, folklore...

In the UK we are blessed with some wonderful mountain toponyms: Helvellyn and Crinkle Crags, Tryfan and Elidir Fawr, Lochnagar and Ladhar Bheinn (Larven)... What would you rather climb? France's Mont Blanc or Mont Sarkozy? Ireland's Purple Mountain or Oscar Wilde Mountain? Scotland's Ben Nevis or Ben Bonar Law (the 1920s Prime Minister)? Let us give the mountains names befitting a timespan that long predates and will long outdate the comparatively petty concerns of homo sapiens.

39

The Chain Gang

IT TAKES A special kind of person to be a top rock climber and, as I describe in *Seconds Away*, I failed to make the cut. Yet the act of moving vertically on rock with space beneath one's feet can be incredibly exhilarating, and the inner mountaineer in me still hankers after a close encounter of the third kind with a big Alpine north face. If only safety concerns, lack of skill and fear of falling could be removed from the equation...

But wait! Those dastardly foreigners have found a way that they can! They festoon great walls and ridges with metal ladders, rungs, chains, wires and ropes that render passage completely safe, no matter how difficult the move or how vast the void below. The Italians call these engineered routes *vie ferrate* (literally, iron roads).

On a *via ferrata* the hardware is attached to the rock, not to you. It is not there to help you climb the route, it is the route itself. Clip yourself on to a chain or the rung of a ladder, using a karabiner attached to a waist loop, and it is amazing what you will try. You will dangle unmoved over enormous drops and climb ladders hundreds of feet high. Of course, it is not for everyone, and requires due care and attention to hardware management, but legions of hillgoers find it an addictive experience.

In the Dolomites, many rock faces that would otherwise be the preserve of rock climbers have been made passable to hillwalkers by the construction of *vie ferrate*. Two of my favourite routes are in the Canazei area: the beautiful Santner Pass and the fascinating Paternkofel, which incorporates a steep 600m-long rock tunnel built to protect soldiers during World War One. In the Brenta, committed scramblers can undertake multi-day hut-to-hut tours across huge rock faces on classic *vie ferrate* such as the Bocchette Way.

The main ridge of the High Tatras, as sharp and difficult as that of the Cuillin, has been draped with ironmongery to facilitate its passage. In the nearby Slovak Paradise National Park, a number of equally exciting routes have been built to enable the negotiation of the region's tortuous gorges. In the South African Drakensberg, the 10,000ft plateau above the Amphitheatre in Royal Natal National Park would be unreachable without a high-altitude rock climb were it not for a couple of airy chain ladders, 100 rungs high, affixed to the cliffs that guard the plateau rim.

Even Yosemite Valley in California, perhaps the world's most famous climbing enclave, has room for one *via ferrata* that puts the summit of mighty Half Dome within the reach of most. Every day in summer, dozens if not hundreds of hikers make the ascent of the steep granite slabs of the northeast face, thanks to a 900ft 'cableway' of wire handrails and wooden crossboards.

Vie ferrate are more thrilling and satisfying than any amusement park ride, so it is a pity there are none in the UK. Why should we have to go abroad to experience their excitements? Why should all our national rock be the preserve of rock climbers? In Scotland there are hundreds of mountains and thousands of rock faces. Is an occasional *via ferrata* too much to ask for? If mountains can be extensively engineered for skiing, surely there is room for a spot of less obtrusive ironmongery for an equally valid mountain pursuit?

Is there not room for one single *via ferrata* among the mile-long, 2,000ft-high cliffs of Ben Nevis, to make at least one tiny portion of Britain's greatest cliff face available to those without rock climbing skills? Is there not room for one single *via ferrata* somewhere in the Cuillin – that great outpouring of rock that is so like the High Tatras?

If such proposals are too leading-edge for the traditionalist lobby, an alternative would be to build *vie ferrate* close to areas that have already been compromised by the machinery of skiing. Next door to the skiers' playground of Coire Cas on Cairn Gorm, for instance, lies Coire an t-Sneachda, whose cliffs provide ideal

On the Santner Pass via ferrata

via ferrata material. If this lone corrie was developed as a *via ferrata* centre, it could become the Acadia of Europe and transform the economy of Aviemore.

Acadia National Park is an island of great granite domes that rise from the sea in northeast USA. Here, landowners have competed to construct the most spectacular *via ferrata*. The *pièce de résistance* is the Precipice Walk, a spectacularly exciting route that works a labyrinthine way up the craggy east face of Champlain Mountain from sea level to the 1,058ft summit.

Hikers come from all over to experience the *via ferrata* playground that is Acadia. Could we not do the same for Aviemore? No, say the fun police, the northern corries of Cairn Gorm must remain inviolate. But why? Can we not, in the whole of Scotland, put aside one single confined mountain space as a year-round adventure playground for all?

Unconvinced? Then try out a *via ferrata* for yourself. The UK does at last possess a couple, built as commercial ventures by Vertical Descents at Honister Pass in the Lake District in 2007 and at the Grey Mare's Tail waterfall near Fort William on the west coast of Scotland in 2014.

There's also the free, sea-level Chain Walk, which rounds Kincraig Point at Earlsferry in Fife. It's not an undertaking on the scale of those mentioned above, but it has its moments, especially with a high tide beneath your feet. If you find you have a penchant for this kind of thing, you'll finish it grinning from ear to ear and wanting more.

Why not build more? A small portion of the taxes paid into quangos such as Scottish Natural Heritage would easily fund development. If not, are there no enterprising landowners out there who would like to attract more cash to their coffers? Isn't it time the UK joined the chain gang?

40

A Summit For All

WHO COULD POSSIBLY object to a railway line that links Perth to Inverness, the Lowlands to the Highlands? Back in 1863, when the line was opened, preservationists did. They were appalled at the very idea of trains running through what was then wild and car-less country, especially the section over Drumochter Pass between Blair Atholl and Dalwhinnie. The mood was captured by the academic and poet Principal Shairp, who wrote of the trains:

Nay! Whate'er of good they herald,
Whereso' comes that hideous roar,
The old charm is disenchanted,
The old Highlands are no more.

You could imagine Shairp waxing equally eloquent against the Cairn Gorm funicular railway, which finally opened in 2001 despite continuing protests. The funicular is the latest in more than a century of proposed Highland mountain railways, and it attracted (and continues to attract) as much opposition as the Drumochter line, the Kyle line and almost all other Highland railways once did. Victorian opposition to these lines now seems excessive. In 100 years' time, will current objections to the Cairn Gorm funicular be viewed in the same way?

The building of railway lines to mountain tops has a long and proud history, replete with great feats of engineering that have opened up the heights to those who are unable, for one reason or another, to get there under their own steam.

In Germany, trains climb the Wendelstein and the Zugspitze, the country's highest mountain. In Switzerland they run up the Rigi and the Rothorn. In the Pyrenees, a train reaches the summit of La Rhune in Basque country. In the United States, trains climb Mount Washington, the highest mountain in New England, and Pikes Peak, one of Colorado's fourteeners. Closer to home, they run up Snowdon in North Wales and Snaefell on the Isle of Man. None of these lines detracts from the stature of the mountains. In fact, I would argue that they add to it.

Since its opening in 1896, the Snowdon Railway has become a much-loved feature of the mountain. Wherever you are on Snowdon, the toot of the train whistle always brings a smile to the face, while even the summit café, splendidly rebuilt in 2009, can seem like nirvana after a tiring ascent. And how many childhood ascents by train have inspired a future generation of hillwalkers?

Scotland had to wait for more than a century to catch up with Wales, and even then protesters forced the owners into a ridiculous compromise. The train was allowed to run to an enlarged Ptarmigan restaurant on the shoulder of Cairn Gorm, c.150m below the summit, but hillwalkers were no longer allowed to enter the building nor passengers leave it. During the skiing season, when skiers had of necessity to be set free, transportation of ice axes and crampons was banned in order to dissuade sneaky walkers. Such a 'closed system' was a recipe for financial disaster, and so it proved.

In 2009 the funicular had to be taken into public ownership. The Ptarmigan was given a Walkers' Entrance. Now, anyone who has walked up is allowed into the hallowed interior to use the facilities and optionally take the train down. The door is secreted around the back, like a tradesman's entrance. Ring the bell and wait to be allowed in. Further progress was made in 2010, when it became possible to take the train up and pay for a guided walk to Cairn Gorm summit.

Yet still, as of 2014, no one who takes the train up is allowed out of Fortress Ptarmigan. In five years, £26.75 million of public money has been pumped into the scheme and it remains a white elephant. In June 2014 ownership again passed to a private company that has progressive development plans. One can only hope.

For too long the agenda of the Cairn Gorm debate has been set by scaremongering preservationists who shelter under the more politically correct umbrella of conservationism. If some of them had their way, they'd do more than preserve the status quo, they'd set the clock back as far as it takes to prevent all mountain access except by 'the long walk-in'. Some would even bar private transport from using the road from Aviemore up to the funicular. With that kind of attitude, it's no wonder Scotland continues to slip down the European league of tourism-related earnings.

The Luddites are well organised, shout loudly and get more than their fair share of press attention, but that doesn't make them right. Their main stated concern is that an influx of visitors would ruin the fragile ecosystem of the Cairn Gorm-Ben Macdui plateau, but behind this environmentally sensitive façade lurks the blinkered self-interest of a few self-important minority groups. It is no coincidence that many of these people are physically able, often live close by and would dearly love to keep the Cairngorms to themselves for their own pursuits.

One of the reasons the ecosystem is fragile is that flora such as blaeberries and fauna such as snow buntings exist here at the limit of their viability, either because of altitude or climate.

Cairn Gorm's northern corries

Well, there are plenty of blaeberries elsewhere, and twitchers would do well to concern themselves more with the potentially devastating effects of global climate change, which by some estimates will clear the last vestiges of Arctic tundra (and snow buntings) from the plateau within a few decades anyway. It sometimes seems that birds have more rights than people.

What seems to have escaped the notice of the objectors is that the vast majority of the people who wish to use the funicular wish to walk precisely *nowhere* on the plateau. The summit of Cairn Gorm lies 150m above the top station and the plateau lies at the foot of an awkward 150m gravelly descent on the far side. Few day-tripping picnickers are likely to go there. In any case, in the unlikely event of an excessive number of visitors becoming a problem, it would be a simple task to introduce a quota system of the kind that works well in many other parts of the world. There is already a booking system for large groups of walkers on Ben Nevis.

Because the preservationists have set the agenda of the debate for years, we tend to overlook the fact that the most endangered of all Cairngorms species is the human being. Perhaps it's time we stood up and championed the rights of man.

On a personal note, a few decades ago I caught reactive arthritis from some dodgy food, which left me crippled and facing the prospect of never being able to walk again. On my darkest days I consoled myself with the fact that I would still be able to ride up Snowdon, but if only there was a Scottish mountain top I could reach…

Let people count in the debate. Let tourists count. Let the people of Speyside, who depend for their livelihood on tourism-related earnings, count. Above all, let the disabled, the elderly and children count. The funicular is not a problem, it is an opportunity. Why are we preserving the Cairngorms at all if not for people? Why not build a wheelchair-accessible path to the top?

Let those who cannot reach the heights under their own steam be able to enjoy what the rest of us take for granted. Let there be one summit that isn't just for the 'intrepid', that isn't just for those who are lucky enough to be able to walk there. Let there be one Scottish Munro that all can enjoy.

41

Ribbons of Stone

AS AN INCREASING percentage of the Scottish countryside comes under the auspices of bodies such as the National Trust for Scotland (NTS), the John Muir Trust (JMT) and Scottish Natural Heritage (SNH), the management of Scottish wild land is becoming increasingly well-meaning but at the same time increasingly obtrusive. There is a danger, increased by the proliferation of visitor honeypots such as national parks and long-distance footpaths, that parts of Scotland will become as regimented an outdoor experience as much of England and Wales.

The formerly prevailing view of wild land management was famously expressed in the 1930s by Percy Unna, a former president of the Scottish Mountaineering Club. He believed that 'the land should be maintained in its primitive condition for all time,' and that 'the hills (should) not be made easier or safer to climb'. To this end, 'paths should not be extended or improved' and 'new paths should not be made'.

His exact words are important, because they became the terms under which he gifted money to the NTS for the purchase of land such as Glen Coe, Kintail and Ben Lawers. But what value his sentiments now, as wild land management becomes increasingly interventionist and the construction of mountain paths rapidly seems to be becoming a bureaucratic imperative? The easier you make a path, the more people will use it. In 2013, according to the British Mountaineering Council (BMC), nearly half a million people were attracted to Snowdon's increasingly manicured paths, which was a huge 23 per cent increase on the previous year alone. Accidents to ill-prepared people increased accordingly. The solution of the park authority? Rewild all secondary paths that may lead astray. This is regimentation at its worst and is rightly labelled 'misguided' by the BMC. What is required is better outdoor education.

The epidemic of path building that began in England and Wales is now spreading unchecked north of the border. Major engineering schemes such as the Ben Nevis Tourist Path and the West Highland Way are just the tip of the iceberg. Above the Ptarmigan restaurant on the shoulder of Cairn Gorm, an artificial rock slide of a path, complete with blue rope handrails and increasingly polished and slippery when wet, snakes ingloriously to the summit. The handrails are required to constrain struggling walkers, who would otherwise take to the easier ground that lies for hundreds of metres to either side.

On Ben Lomond, a nine-year path engineering project in the 1990s involved the shifting of 150 tonnes of stone, including the laying of 200 metres of stone pitching that amounts to nothing short of a rock staircase up an otherwise wonderful swathe of grassy hillside. If this is what hillwalking is to be reduced to, we might as well stay at home and climb the stairs. The project cost £340,000, of which £200,000 came from Scottish Natural Heritage.

Also in the 1990s, SNH granted £100,000 per year for three years for work on the West Highland Way. In 1998 it granted £63,000 to the Queen for work on Balmoral paths. The Ben Nevis Tourist Path continues to eat up tens if not hundreds of thousands of pounds. Unelected quangos such as SNH, with public money to spend, can be notoriously profligate. You and I, as taxpayers, paid for all these paths and had no choice in the matter.

Another SNH contribution was to the re-engineering of the Stac Pollaidh path, a scheme additionally supported by a grant of £256,000 from the Heritage Lottery Fund. Is this what lottery money should be used for? Is it even wise to make it easier for unwary tourists to reach the difficult summit ridge of Stac Pollaidh?

All this work is necessary, say the new countryside commissars, to combat path erosion. But a path by definition is eroded. It has been eroded into existence by the passage of man or animal. And *whatever* state of erosion it is in, it rarely impacts on the environment. Paths are nearly always minuscule waymarks on great expanses of mountainside, as an aerial view will confirm. Even a path as wide as 25m, as the old Ben Lomond path was measured to be at one point, has infinitesimal impact on the total environment and ecology of a mountain.

Only in very special cases, such as when a traverse path destabilises a whole hillside, is there a wider impact. Such a case is in evidence at the Grey Mare's Tai in the Borders, whose path was re-engineered at a cost of £100,000, but more often than not there are no environmental or safety considerations whatsoever.

A more telling reason for the current obsession with path-building becomes clear if you read the literature put out by the various countryside bodies, which all seem to suffer from *ugly scar* syndrome. 'Ugly scar' is the pejorative term by which they refer to paths of which they disapprove, and euphemisms such as path restoration, improvement and renovation are the terms by which they refer to large-scale works of earth movement that from a Percy Unna viewpoint might be considered acts of institutionalised vandalism.

Cairn Gorm summit path

Ugliness, like beauty, lies in the eye of the beholder. The new paths are also scars, in which it is difficult to see any superior beauty. At the time of writing, the rubbly path up Braeriach in the Cairngorms is being re-engineered as a series of rock staircases linked by steep gravel chutes whose ballbearing-like consistency is a menace. A few zigzags would help. The old path was rough, but more natural and certainly easier to ascend and descend. How can such engineered scars ever be less ugly than natural scars created by animals or humans?

The path up to Coire Lagan in the Cuillin used to be a whole series of parallel paths. The ugly scar brigade measured at one point 22 parallel strands over a range of 40m. So what? Some people have a problem with heights; path builders seem to have a problem with widths.

Some of us loved that beautiful, characterful, peaty, multi-lane highway to the heights, which had developed over more than a century of approaches to classic Cuillin climbs. It was a privilege to walk in the footsteps of great pioneers of Scottish mountaineering such as Norman Collie and John McKenzie.

Then the engineers moved in, destroyed the old tracks forever and channelled everyone onto the increasingly ubiquitous, artificial, regimented, follow-my-leader boulderway. So much for freedom to roam.

Another 'ugly scar', according to the literature of the John Muir Trust, was the old path up Schiehallion, which was replaced at a cost of a few hundred thousand pounds and requires (as they all do) continued maintenance. Although the old path became boggy in parts after heavy rain, on a sunny summer's day the soft peat sections provided a wonderfully springy and joyful descent... which raises perhaps the most important issue of all.

The footbed of naturally evolved paths contrasts sharply with that of most engineered paths, whose slabs and gravel are potentially more likely to cause injury. The problem is not confined to increasingly worn and slippery cobbles such as those on Cairn Gorm. Hillwalking puts enough strain on knee joints as it is. Artificial steps force the hillwalker into unnatural foot placements that exacerbate this strain.

The worst culprits are the stone staircases that increasingly litter our mountainsides. Stepping up onto a flat rock, rather than a sloping hillside, drastically increases muscle effort, knee-joint articulation and joint wear. No wonder many walkers choose to walk beside the staircases rather than on them. On descent, especially when wet, they can even be dangerous unless tackled with care – ask fell runners.

In the 1990s, walkers were canvassed for their views on new paths up Ben A'an and Ben Ledi, and they evinced little concern for path conditions as long as they avoided wet feet. On the extensively engineered Ben A'an path, 36 per cent still walked beside it in places. A few stepping stones, drainage ditches and cross drains to channel water run-off would satisfy most walkers' requirements. On Ben Lomond, such a minimalist approach to improving the Ptarmigan path has produced a much more enjoyable route to the summit than the far more expensive main path.

With more tourists on the mountains than in Percy Unna's day, there may well be a case for a network of manicured paths up a selection of popular mountains such as Snowdon, Ben Nevis and Ben Lomond. And by all means let's build some paths suitable for disabled access, as in other parts of the world. Not all of the new paths are regrettable. There are wonderful new paths, for instance, in Cairn Gorm's corries and around Derry Lodge and Ben Lawers. But we should question what appears to have become the default position that all old paths are ugly scars in need of costly remedial work. Otherwise, the uncoordinated pathbuilding bandwagon will continue to roll unchecked over our wild land and change it forever.

We need a concerted plan and an improved set of construction guidelines. Here are two commendable guidelines used on the Appalachian Trail in the eastern USA: (1) build gentle switchbacks (zigzags) rather than steep fall-line rock staircases wherever possible, (2) always place the emphasis on producing an *attractive walkway*.

Are such guidelines applicable on UK terrain? Is the current state of the art in path engineering up to the job? Should we be spending vast sums of public money on it? Or should we stand with Percy Unna and say: send the path builders home to think again. A public debate on the issue is long overdue, but such is the de facto pro-interventionist path construction lobby that there is no forum for such a debate. Meanwhile, staircases continue to proliferate. If no action is taken soon, it may be too late to save our mountains from permanent disfigurement and ageing hillwalkers from painful knee damage.

42

The Psychology of Risk

IN NORTHERN CANADA, a road crosses a railway line at right angles. There is no gate and no signal to warn of the approach of an infrequent train. Blanket forest used to make it impossible for a car driver to see any distance along the line before he reached it. To improve sight lines, a diamond-shaped clearing was cut into the forest, opening up the view to left and right along the line.

Now that they could see further, drivers responded by approaching the crossing at higher speeds, thereby lengthening braking distance, and eventually there was a fatal accident when a vehicle was hit by a train. As a result, the clearing was expanded so that drivers could see even further to left and right. The result? They now approached the crossing at even greater speeds. Despite attempts to improve safety, the risk of an accident remained the same.

The tactic employed by the drivers is known as risk compensation, in which a perceived safer environment is counterbalanced by riskier behaviour. People behave in this way because, although capacity for risk may vary from person to person, for any one individual it remains constant – a phenomenon known as risk homeostasis.

It is for this reason that attempts to reduce road accidents by enforcing the wearing of seat belts don't work. Seat belts merely make drivers feel safer, which causes them to compensate by driving with less care. All that strapping someone into a car does is change the nature of accidents, with drivers now being less injured than other road users (although global data suggest there can be more driver deaths too).

In the UK, accident numbers did indeed reduce when seat belts became compulsory in 1983, but only because of a parallel campaign against drunk driving (the reduction in deaths occurred between 10pm and 4am). Following the introduction of compulsory child seat belts in 1989, child deaths actually rose by ten per cent. Despite currently perceived wisdom, studies that compare accident rates before and after the introduction of seat belt laws, and between countries that do and do not have such laws, show no reduction in accident incidence from the wearing of seat belts. Nor should any be expected. If you really want to reduce road deaths, make driving more *unsafe* for the driver by placing a spike on the steering column, pointing at his chest. That'll alter his risk compensation analysis a tad.

The same psychology of risk applies on mountains. The development of camming devices for belays in the 1960s enabled harder routes to be tackled. Portable oxygen enabled Himalayan mountaineers to go higher and eventually climb Everest. Fixed ropes now enable more people to climb (and die on) the world's highest mountain.

Path improvements entice people on to the hill who might previously have considered it too risky, as do weather reports, GPS gadgets, mobile phone coverage and even the availability in the UK of free mountain rescue. Improvements in crampon and ice axe technology have made harder ice climbs possible. I still recall purchasing my first pair of crampons and marvelling at the novelty of being able to stand firm on inclined ice.

Every year climbers and hillwalkers are injured or die on mountains and, no matter what 'safety' measures are introduced, this will always be the case. A mountain can be a dangerous place, but so can the home. More people die from accidents in a house than on a mountain. In Japan in 2011, three times more people died in a bathtub than in a road accident.

Making the mountains safer is not the answer because, be you as risk-averse as a Howard Hughes or as risk-loving as a Grand Canyon slack-liner, your risk profile remains constant.

The only way to reduce mountain accidents is to enforce restrictions, and there are those who would do so. If certain *high hied yins* had their way, we would not be allowed on the hill until we had passed a mountaincraft course, completed a fitness training schedule, bought the latest hi-tech clothing and over-priced footwear, stocked up on emergency bivouac equipment and survival rations, planned and memorised all the mileages, altitudes and compass bearings of every section of our route and preferably hired the services of a professional mountain guide.

There are even those who, following the spate of deaths in recent Scottish winters, would ban people from venturing on to the hills in the first place. Don't believe this could never happen.

Already there are 'snow gates' in Scotland on the A82 and A9, preventing access from the south to the prime winter climbing areas of Glen Coe and the Cairngorms. The gates close the roads to all traffic, no matter how well equipped a vehicle is for winter conditions.

The state has never been reticent in encroaching on individual liberty in order to make us 'safer'. Until 1976, motorcyclists never thought that wearing a helmet would become compulsory. Now, only Sikhs are legally permitted to ride helmet-free. An equivalent helmet law is occasionally mooted for pedal cyclists and rock climbers. In Canada and the USA, climbers have been banned from some crags for not wearing helmets, although the policy had to be dropped in the USA because of policing difficulties.

Surely, as long as no one else's safety is at risk, it is up to each of us to decide the level of risk we are willing to take. On a British hill at least, my own risk profile dictates a few simple personal rules to follow. Don't rely on a forecast of good weather and leave waterproofs behind. Don't follow a higher-risk taker beyond your comfort zone. Always be prepared to turn back. In the final analysis, life ends in one way only, but I'm not ready for that yet. Staying alive is not the coward's way out. But it is important that I, not the state, make the decision.

The right to climb mountains is not just an issue of freedom of access and of safety but also of personal freedom and responsibility. The last person by whom I want to be saved is a well-meaning but misguided soul who insists on acting as the arbiter of my wellbeing. And, as a sentient being, the last person from whom I want to be saved is myself.

Carpe Diem

43

Bothy Extracts

MOUNTAIN HUTS ARE a feature of many of the world's mountain ranges, but Scottish Highland bothies are unique. A tumultuous history, punctuated with famines and forced evictions, saw the Highlands cleared of people in the 18th and 19th centuries, and this left countless habitations to go to ruin. Some of these have been converted into 'bothies' to provide basic shelter in the wilds.

None provide more than Spartan refuge but they can also save lives. In a roaring Cairngorms blizzard that ripped our tent wide open, Judith and I would have been in a parlous situation had not Corrour Bothy come to our rescue. It was dirty, packed and uncomfortable that night, but never had we less cause for complaint.

Fading logbooks, dating back to the early 20th century, give an insight into the esteem in which the old bothy, now renovated, was held. Entries these days tend to be of the 'Kilroy was here' variety. In former times, when the remote Cairngorms attracted a more select and committed group of aficionados, entries tended to be more poetic, more amusing and more enthused with 'the spirit of the hills'. They evoke a time when, before the explosion of outdoor pursuits in the past half-century, and the advent of easy access and modern gear, being in the hills was a more deeply appreciated privilege.

Here are some examples taken from the old Corrour Bothy logbooks, now tattered and torn, written by anonymous authors long gone. Many thanks to all of them. May their spirit never be forgotten.

Magnificent scenery, enchanting mists – and soaking rain. What scenery, what weather! What pleasures can match those of the unorthodox insanities of the lovers of the high places, the magnificent madness of the mountaineer? Yet thousands hit a pill across a park or tup a hollow rubber sphere across a net and call it sport! Ye Gods! (21/7/30)

Met report: 17/10 cloud. Visibility: 0. Epicentre of earthquake half a mile up the glen. Avalanches and landslides intermittent. Water vapour content of air: 93 per cent. Wind velocity: 104mph, with gusts rising to 148mph. 3cwt boulders blowing down the glen make walking difficult. (6/8/51)

There was a young lady of Ballater
Who went for a dip in Loch Callater
Her natatory prowess
She started to showess
Then up came a monster and Swallater. (24/9/38)

In the true tradition of the nature reserve, we gave protection to approximately 50 per cent of Scotland's midges last night. (18/8/66)

There is sure no place like this... this side of hell. (19/9/31)

Time on our hands led to experiments in cooking. Hit on the following recipe:

> Half tin corned beef
> Half tin baked beans (small)

Mash up well together. Add quarter cup water with third cup Oxo. Add oatmeal until fairly stiff and fry the whole damned issue in plenty of fat. Then dig a hole at a safe distance from the bothy and bury the lot. (8/8/39)

Back once more to Corrour, which I find silent and empty. Alone I sit beside the fire and my thoughts shift over the hills. Few realise how many more things one sees and hears in the

Bothy life

hills, alone. The wind is rising, so I close tightly both doors and replenish the dying fire. The candles burn brightly while outside black night courses on. (19/10/30)

To come from the white-clad slopes of our beloved hills, having drunk deep at the well of knowledge and beauty... And sit by the fire till the spirit of the bothy enshrines itself round our hearts... To feel that we have worked and our wages are taken. And to sink into peaceful slumber in some place like this... And know that we are not dead. (3/1/31)

Alone I climb
The rugged hills that lead me out of time. (26/8/28)

For go I must
But come I must
And if men ask you why,
You may put the blame
On the stars and the sun
And the dark hills and the sky. (22/9/30)

At the moment there are five of us, but the weakest will probably succumb before morning and the bodies will make fine seats and provide food for the survivors. (1/1/39)

Pity we can't stay another day, when the scarf Bill is knitting would be big enough to re-roof the bothy. (25/9/39)

No sunshine falls on the bothy walls,
Nought but the wind and rain,
But our spirits soar as the Primi roar,
For we'll soon have dinner again. (6/8/28)

Having eventually got a magnificent fire going, a Czechoslovakian gentleman of unknown parentage set about extinguishing it by drying all his gear. (4/8/66)

Tonight we have a fire. A magnificent fire. In its fiercest moments it has driven us to the back of the bothy. Even Jim, the Asbestos Wonder, was driven before its power. Shirts have been abandoned and even the door has been opened to temper the boiler-room atmosphere. Phew! (5/1/38)

Wanted – Haggis Beaters. Assemble on top of Cairn Toul at 2am to be issued with orders. Prospective beaters should be able to hit a haggis at 40 yards with a loaded kilt. (20/8/66)

Oh for a minister to save my sole,
It's parting company with my boot. (18/7/38)

HOWF RAL OVR FRAM HOWF ALSES FAM
HOWF AST HOWF LEIT OVR DAIE
HOWF IXED OVR FYTE IN FUTVR STATE
HOWF EW CYM BAC 2 SAIE. (19/9/31)

Best of luck and a safe return from the war to all those mountaineers who are forced to go and fight on either side (4/1/40)

Came over the pass today with a Londoner who told me in course of conversation that the Lairig Ghru is the finest pass in England. He made several remarks equally blasphemous and was lucky to get past this place alive. (30/5/39)

There was a young lady from Spain,

Who when climbing the Cairngorms in rain,
Would first climb the peaks
Than strip off her breeks,
And shout 'I'm insane, I'm insane'. (14/8/56)

We think we may have climbed Ben Macdui but, owing to the atmospheric conditions, hell knows where we've been. (1/9/39)

I was chased by a bogey all the way from the highest summit of Braeriach down to the Lairig where I think it lost me among the boulders. It was a horrid grey thing and it really made me frightened. I am serious and shivering with fright. (25/7/55)

Just passing through... The Grey Man (15/9/58)

Please leave a Christmas dinner for the mice. They are very friendly. (25/12/52)

It occurs to me that Corrour will provide future archaeologists with a unique opportunity for discovering long-lost facts concerning the twentieth century: 'Today we dug up from the floor of Corrour ruin an ice axe head circa 1960'. (21/5/66)

Back again. Good Heavens. Swore I would never come here again. Wet clothes. Sore feet. What a life! (5/5/40)

44

Hiking in Clan and Tribal Country

CENTURIES AGO, there was a society that lived close to the land, in tune with the rhythms of nature. The people had food aplenty and prospered in their way, but it was a feudal society, with strong allegiances to the chief. The men were often conscripted to follow him into battle against rival clans. Many great warriors died, and tales of their deeds were handed down across the generations to become part of oral history.

After many hundreds of years, the clans buried their differences and banded together to fight a superior neighbour who spoke a different language, but they were overrun. Their homes were burned to the ground, their customs and traditions proscribed, their livelihood taken from them and their land given over to incomers with new methods of exploiting it. Survivors who did not adapt to the new reality were driven from their homeland to seek new lives elsewhere.

In the succeeding years, the descendants of those who stayed behind became assimilated into the new society that evolved. But nostalgia for the old days remains. Some still campaign for independence and look back on the old chiefs as almost mythical heroes.

No, this land is not Highland Scotland, it is North America, and the society in question is that of the indigenous Americans who lived there before the white man came and called them Red Indians. Comparisons with the Highlands are striking. In 2008, the Scottish Crofting Foundation even produced a report asking the United Nations to grant Highlanders the same rights as Native Americans by recognising them as the 'indigenous peoples of the Highlands and Islands'.

Apaches and Comanches hated each other as much as Campbells and Macdonalds but, unlike in Scotland, the vast open spaces of North America provided room for all and food for all. The bulwark of this society was the buffalo, as plentiful as herring once were off the west coast of Scotland. A single herd could number millions and take days to pass. To catch them, braves would 'run' them on horseback to a cliff and drive them over the edge to their deaths. The tradition is commemorated at heritage sites such as Head-Smashed-In-Buffalo Jump in Alberta.

The nearest Scottish equivalent to the buffalo was the red deer, which was also hunted in huge numbers across the Highlands. Deer survive to this day on the great sporting estates, but the great herds of buffalo fared less well. In the course of little more than a decade in the 19th century, disease, fire, drought and outright slaughter reduced their numbers from millions to a few hundred. It was this, as much as the white man's western expansion, that put an end to the traditional Native American way of life.

Out of choice or necessity, many Scots left home and found adventure in the American West. Sir William Stewart of Murthly, for instance, decorated for bravery at the Battle of Waterloo, became a prominent mountain man who spent many years hunting and trapping in the Rocky Mountains. He even shipped buffalo back to the grounds of his Perthshire estate, together with three Native Americans who found the local firewater an unexpected challenge. One drunken evening, they fixed wheels to a large rowboat, hitched buffalo to it and galloped through the streets of Dunkeld with whooping war cries. What a sight that must have been to the god-fearing townsfolk.

James Mackay from Sutherland discovered the source of the Mississippi River. Robert Stuart from Callander became the third person to canoe across the breadth of the continent. James Macleod from Skye helped found Canada's Northwest Mounted Police. William Keith from Aberdeenshire became a great painter of the Californian wilderness. His friend John Muir, from Dunbar, loved the Rocky Mountains so much that he became instrumental in the formation of the world's first national park, Yellowstone, in 1872.

In 1876, Native Americans made their last great stand at the Battle of the Little Big Horn, where General Custer was killed. Less than 20 years later, in a surreal twist of fate, legendary frontiersman Buffalo Bill was re-enacting the battle in Glasgow. The 'redskins' were cast as the villains and their number included Native American chiefs such as Kicking Bear and Short Bull, who had taken part in the actual battle.

So successful was Buffalo Bill's Wild West touring show that he returned with an even bigger extravaganza in 1894, when it is recorded that he attended a Glasgow Rangers football match and Annie 'Get Your Gun' Oakley learned to ride a bike. Such is progress.

Large tracts of land in North America are still owned by various tribes, who nowadays are more exercised in building casinos to relieve the white man of his cash rather than his scalp. On a lesser scale of enterprise, 'friendly Indian' stores dot the dusty western highways, selling Native American artefacts. Go to an historic site such as Canyon de Chelly, where ancient rock dwellings stand in natural alcoves half-way up sheer canyon walls, and you are likely to be approached by a denim-clad Navajo who, for a certain sum, will offer to guide you to a secret location littered with old arrowheads he swears are genuine.

Thanks to the size of the country, the lack of development on most Native American land, and the expanding number of national parks, much of the American West remains inviolate and is a magical place to explore on foot. The Rocky Mountain rambler will occasionally come across old mines and dwellings, but they have been assimilated into the vast landscape. Hiking in the more confined glens and corries of the Scottish Highlands has a different vibe. Reminders of former, more populous, times are everywhere, from ancient trails to battle sites, from dilapidated crofts and shielings to grand castles that are still inhabited.

As Steven Pinker demonstrates in his book *The Better Angels of Our Nature: Why Violence Has Declined*, the world is a nicer place now, with less war and less killing. It is now possible to wander the wild places of Scotland and the American West, and revel in their peace and solitude, without fear of speaking English. But what should never be forgotten is the tragic history that has made these lands as they are. As Dr Johnson wrote after visiting the Highlands in 1773: 'Far from me be such frigid philosophy as may conduct us indifferent and unmoved over any ground which has been dignified by wisdom, bravery or virtue.'

45

The Wisdom of Chief Joseph

AT THREE O'CLOCK precisely, in the sleepy little town of Joseph, Oregon, they rob the bank. While ordinary, peace-lovin' towns-folk go about their daily business (the men in placket-front shirts, the women in crinolined skirts), three desperadoes ride down Main Street and hitch their horses to a rail. Spurs jangling, hands poised above gun holsters, they mosey down to the corner of 2nd Street and enter the bank. For a moment all is quiet, then a woman screams and gunshots ring out.

From behind me, the sheriff starts shooting. His deputy, up on the roof, joins in. Across the wide expanse of Main Street the gunfight rages. Two baddies bite the dust, but then the tide turns. The deputy's body lands beside me and outlaw Cyrus Fitzhugh makes it back to his horse with the money and high-tails it out of town.

As if this isn't startling enough, a descendant of Chief Joseph is riding through town, resplendent on his magnificent pinto, his spectacularly feathered headdress gleaming brilliantly in the sun. And palefaces are actually applauding. It is a poignant moment, for Chief Joseph and his tribe of Perces Nez Indians were chased from their homeland here in 1877 and attacked in a series of 13 battles all the way up to the Canadian border.

On the edge of town there is even a tipi village, where a free Friendship Feast is being held by some of the 'indigenous peoples' (as they wish to be called). The angular outlines of the closely grouped tipis form stunning geometrical patterns, like white sails against the blue sky.

The ritual ride through town of Chief Joseph's descendant heralds the start of an eagerly awaited parade that is the climax of Chief Joseph Days, the high point of the local calendar. It takes two hours for the 150-or-so 'acts' to file past. They include floats, stagecoaches, rodeo queens, posses of riders and even Boy Blue, 'the Brahmin steer that thinks it's a horse'. One wonders what the persecuted old chief would make of all this, in the town now named after him.

The Fall of 1996 marked the centenary of the original bank robbery and it was agreed that the year's daily re-enactments were even more stirring than usual. Sadly, the spectacle ended a few years later because the ranch hands who played the various roles had more important duties to attend to. But the strange, true story of the robbery and its aftermath continues to resonate.

Dave Tucker, one of the three outlaws, was shot three times but survived. He spent several years in jail, saw the error of his ways and later actually became vice president of the bank he had helped to rob. Cyrus Fitzhugh disappeared with the loot into the snow-dusted mountain country around Hell's Canyon and was never caught. Perhaps he perished in the wilderness, or maybe he made it through the Wallowa Mountains north of Joseph, managed to cross the treacherous Snake River in Hell's Canyon and survived the Seven Devils Range of Idaho on the far side.

Both ranges are nearly 10,000ft (3,000m) high. The highest peak in the Seven Devils is He Devil (9,393ft), while the highest peak in the Wallowas is Sacajawea Peak (9,838ft). The Wallowa Mountains are protected as the Eagle Cap Wilderness, named for its most prominent if slightly lower 9,572ft peak, but it is more colloquially known as Little Switzerland and even boasts its own Matterhorn. Fired by the tales I heard during Chief Joseph Days, I wanted to see what this still roadless country was like, so I shouldered a pack and set out to investigate.

The Seven Devils proved hard to negotiate. There are few trails and the mountains are steep and rugged. Great rock outcrops make cross-country travel awkward. Reaching He Devil's rock pillar summit required bushwhacking through forest and scrub, and scrambling across boulder fields and snow. The summit plinth was an airy perch, far from anywhere. Its logbook informed me that, on that day, 11 July, I was the first person to climb the mountain that year.

On top of Eagle Cap

The Wallowas are a more extensive and scenic range, criss-crossed by a network of trails that make the remote interior more accessible to trekkers. I took the East Lostine River Trail to the achingly pretty Lakes Basin, where pine-shored lakes nestled beneath rugged granite peaks. The colours astounded. At the foot of Eagle Cap, sparkling white icebergs calved into Glacier Lake, which was deep blue in the centre and emerald green around its shores and islets. The more vivid green of its surrounding vegetation contrasted with the red screes and grey crags that towered all around. Lush meadows provided idyllic campsites. A breeze took the edge of the heat and kept the skeeters at bay. Snow melt provided refreshing drinking water. This was prime backpacking country.

The next day, as I stood at the summit of Eagle Cap and surveyed the pristine wilderness at my feet, I recalled the words of a Nez Perce woman who had spoken passionately at the Friendship Feast of two principles that modern society could learn from the old tribal life. The first was infinite renewability – the idea that the earth would survive, with or without us, whatever we do to it. The second was reciprocity – the idea of living in harmony with the earth, never taking from it more than we need, and giving a little back for all that we take.

Chief Joseph was eventually caught just short of the Canadian border. His touching surrender speech, one of the greatest ever recorded, ended with the words: 'I am tired; my heart is sick and sad. From where the sun now stands, I will fight no more forever.' He was taken to Washington, where he enthralled his captors with stirring speeches that still echo around the Friendship Feast. 'Treat all men alike. Give them all an even chance to live and grow. They are all brothers. The earth is the mother of all people.'

I doubt that Cyrus Fitzhugh survived his attempted escape through the Wallowas and Seven Devils. Somewhere out there, his loot may still await discovery by some bemused backpacker. I come away from Joseph and Little Switzerland with stories of Wild West cowboys and Indians, with memories of untouched wilderness, and with new hope that men can live together, in harmony with each other and the environment.

46

Munro Bagging
with Queen Victoria

QUEEN VICTORIA could be a difficult person – interesting people always are. It's a pity that the image of her that has been handed down to posterity, owing to the development of photography in her later life, is of a tubby old woman permanently dressed in black. Age does no favours to anyone.

In her younger days she was a passionate woman, besotted with the love of her life, Prince Albert of Saxe-Coburg-Gotha.

His premature death from typhoid, when they were both aged 42, sucked the life force out of her. Her predilection for black, which she wore for the remaining 40 years of her life, was testament to her undying love for him. His room was kept as if he were still alive. Every night, she still had his clothes laid out for him for the following morning. Every morning, she still had his breakfast made.

Spiritualism was fashionable in the late 19th century and there is cause to believe that Victoria tried to reach Albert through séances. John Brown, the Balmoral gillie to whom she became attached, was said to have psychic powers, and this may have been the reason she came to depend on him following Albert's death. Her granddaughter Alix, who became Tsarina Alexandra of Russia, developed a similar fixation on Rasputin.

While Albert was alive, not even giving birth to nine children could douse Victoria's ardour for him. Some of her treatment of her children is difficult to excuse in the light of modern child rearing practice, but those were different times. She was never cut out to deal with the demands of royal motherhood. Children were simply an impediment to the only relationship she really wanted.

If only she and Albert had understood contraception, her life would have been happier... and perhaps the First World War could even have been averted (the belligerent German Kaiser was her grandson). She refused even to breastfeed, as that part of her body was reserved for Albert. It is not recorded whether she was 'amused' or otherwise about the genital piercing that now bears his name and which gave an elegant line to the tight trousers of the day.

She could be temperamental and wilful, but perhaps that is not surprising given the constraints of her situation. Hers was a life spent longing for escape, from the restrictions of childhood, from the duties of adulthood and from the abyss of bereavement. It was this that drew her back again and again to the Scottish Highlands, where she found precious freedom. She particularly relished her 'great expeditions', as she called them, to the summits of mountains with her beloved 'Bertie'. Many of these were Munros, although the term did not yet exist (Sir Hugh Munro had not yet even been born).

She was an accomplished writer and sketch artist, and her journals are full of her passion for both Albert and the mountains. The couple first visited Scotland in 1841 as youthful 23-year-olds. From London, they journeyed up the east coast by boat to Edinburgh before riding northwest to Loch Tay. Victoria was enchanted by everything: the coastline, the towns, the people, the language and above all the Highland scenery. In her journal, she name-checked every mountain she passed, listing their names like a mantra.

In 1844 they returned and stayed at Blair Castle. Victoria rhapsodised over Glen Tilt ('no description can do it justice') and bagged her first Munro, Carn a' Chlamain (963m), on the glen's northwest side. She rode most of the way to the summit on her pony (as befitting a queen), but had to scramble up the final 30m of quartzite rubble. She left Blair Castle hooked, pining for her 'dear hills'. Carn a' Chlamain was to be the first of many ascents.

In 1847 she and Albert cruised up the west coast before heading inland to Ardverikie House on Loch Laggan, now made famous in certain circles by its use as a set for the television series Monarch of the Glen. The weather was terrible but the scenery was, as ever, 'very beautiful'. The following year they visited Balmoral Castle for the first time and fell in love with that too. 'All seemed to breathe freedom and peace', Victoria wrote. On her pony, 'with the wind blowing a hurricane', she made the first of many ascents of Lochnagar (1,155m), 'the jewel of all mountains here'.

In 1850 she ascended Beinn a' Bhuird (1,197m), not by the easy way from Linn of Quoich, but from Invercauld via Carn Fiaclach, which was translated for her as Tooth's Craig. It was a steep, stony ascent on another cold, windy day, and required more footwork than usual. Undaunted, she still thought that 'the view from the top was magnificent' and all in all it was 'a delightful expedition'.

Lochnagar, Queen Victoria's favourite mountain

So much did she love the Highlands that she became determined to procure a bolthole up there, away from the royal pressure cooker of London. Her first choice was Ardverikie, but the memory of bad weather and midges persuaded her that Balmoral on Deeside, at the foot of Lochnagar, would make a more congenial base. Work on a new house (the present Balmoral Castle) began in 1853 and by 1856 she would write: 'Every year my heart becomes more fixed in this dear Paradise.'

From here, she and Albert climbed Ben Macdui via Glen Derry and Loch Etchachan, a route that was steep and awkward enough to require more walking than riding. On another typical Highland day of mist and 'piercing cold wind', she even laced her water with whisky to combat the chill. Again, she took it all in her stride, recording the scenery as 'so wild, so solitary... truly sublime and impressive'.

Her last great expedition was in 1861, when she crossed the summits of Carn an Tuirc (1,019m) and Cairn of Claise (1,064m) on the plateau east of Glen Shee. It gave her 'such a longing for further Highland expeditions' but, tragically, it was not to be.

Her Bertie died only two months later. She continued to retreat to the Highlands whenever possible, even to the detriment of her royal duties, but could no longer bring herself to climb mountains without him.

In 1865, four years after Albert's death, she returned *incognita* to Taymouth, where they had stayed on their first visit to Scotland. Here, she wandered up a hillside 'not without deep emotion', pining for earlier days when they were 'young and happy'.

There is much to be gained from climbing mountains on one's own, but the experience is intensified if that strange compulsion, so lately discovered by the human race, can be shared with a loving partner. Victoria did not have the happiest of lives but, for a while at least, she was lucky enough to have found her partner, and that is more than some ever do.

> 'For today lit by your laughter, between the crushing years,
> I will chance, in the hereafter, eternities of tears.'

47

Lost Innocence

EVERY TIME I scramble down the Sgumain Stone Shoot on the Isle of Skye, and I pass the foot of Petronella, I think of Mairet. And of what her life might have been. And of what she might have come to mean to me.

The only reminder I have of her is a photograph taken in cloud on some long-forgotten hill top. Her back is to the camera and the hood of her anorak hides her mane of long black hair. You can't even tell it's Mairet. Only I know it is.

She was barely into her 20s. Dundee University Rucksack Club's top female rock climber. Only Ritchie was more acrobatic on rock. Like me, she loved the hills and never missed a club meet, but while I aimed for a summit, she gravitated to a crag. Rock was her love.

As with other colleagues in the club, we came to know each other through long coach trips to the Highlands (few of us owned a car in the 1960s) and boozy après-climb evenings where we discussed the day's derring-do and, in Housman's words, 'cursed whatever brute and blackguard made the world'.

In those pre-feminist days, when girls were supposed to drink martini and lemonade, she sank pints with the boys. She hated to be thought of as a member of the so-called 'weaker' sex. After a hard day on the hill, a quenching pint would soon become three. Outsiders would look at her askance and pass unflattering remarks, and sometimes her anger would boil over and she would confront them for their misogyny. She knew we had her back. She was one of us and we protected our own.

As products of single-sex schools, we were painfully slow to realise we shared a growing attraction that went beyond companionship. I began to see in her a beauty of which, in her desire to be taken seriously as a rugged climber, she seemed oblivious. I related to her sense of adventure, her abandon, her refusal to give any countenance to 'straights' (as we cool young people of the '60s called anyone who wasn't like us).

It took us more than a year of furtive glances to make sense of the mutual signals and take tentative steps to do something about it. We found ourselves hanging out down at Riverside Park beside the River Tay, metaphorically circling each other, essaying conversational gambits. They weren't dates. There was no way I would have been capable of asking Mairet out on a date, and girls certainly didn't ask boys out in those days.

We barely knew how to speak to each other, never mind articulate attraction. We'd meet on the pretext of going for a jog or discussing the next weekend's meet. On one occasion she managed to borrow a bicycle and we took turns on that. And that was all. Our relationship never evolved. We were young and innocent. We had no moves.

At the end of the academic year, we joined the annual

Rucksack Club pilgrimage to the Isle of Skye. We didn't go together, we were just part of the crowd that turned up at Glenbrittle campsite. We all loved the Cuillin. Who wouldn't? To me, the pinnacled ridges and summits were an irresistible lure. For Mairet, the endless, soaring, sun-kissed crags were a spiritual home. I seconded a number of rock climbs, even led a few, but I was never in her league and chance had it that we never found ourselves together on the same rope.

One day she climbed Petronella on the great Coire Lagan face of Sron na Ciche. It was graded Severe in my dog-eared Climbing Guide, but the awkward crack at the start always looked harder to me. Today it is graded Very Severe. Petronella is named for a Scottish dance. I wasn't witness to Mairet's ascent, but I was told later that she had indeed danced up the rock. When she returned to Glen Brittle campsite, her eyes sparkled.

After Skye, like everyone else, we went our separate ways, any latent feelings for each other forever unacknowledged. I would spend the summer tarring North Sea oil pipes to earn money. She would follow her dream.

That dream took her to the Alps. She climbed The Matterhorn and was killed on the way down.

I heard the news when I returned to university for the autumn term. Her parents were in town to meet her friends, but I didn't press them for details. No one knew about our barely acknowledged feelings for each other, so I grieved in private. As far as I know, her body was never found.

I don't pretend that the loss was as great for me as it was for her family and those who knew her more intimately, but she was too young, the same age as I was, both of us on the cusp of life… with so much between us left unsaid.

Now, after all the years in between, those guarded feelings seem to belong to a young man I barely recognise. Life goes on. There are new experiences. More mature relationships. It troubles me that I can't even remember Mairet's last name.

But, my goodness, her face haunts me still.

48

I Keep the Dreams

AFTER 30 YEARS of adventure in the Scottish Highlands, a peculiar thing happened to me. Something I would never have believed possible. I suddenly lost the desire to climb in the Highlands altogether. The mountains had become so familiar to me that they held few surprises any more. Yes, I know they're *always* different. I couldn't understand it either, but somehow I was climbed-out. It had reached the point where I needed an Alp or a Rocky Mountain to get the juices flowing again.

I don't know how long that gap in my résumé would have lasted because after a year or so I met Allan. He was a late starter, just discovering the hills, and his keenness immediately rekindled my own. Before long we had become best friends, off as well as on the hill. Our social lives became intertwined. With his girlfriend Sandi, we formed a regular threesome around town.

And so it came to pass that, in my '50s, I found myself tackling some of the longest and hardest hill walks of my life. Routes I had never before considered within my capabilities would have Allan salivating with anticipation. He was 15 years younger than me and typically made no allowance for it, which was both a compliment and a pain. Any show of reticence on my part would only broaden his grin.

I had climbed Ben Cleuch in the Ochils Range, between Stirling and Perth, many times for exercise. With Allan's infectious, try-anything sense of adventure pushing me to greater ambition, we now walked the entire length of the range from west to east. The greatest number of Munros I had ever climbed in a single day was seven, on the South Glen Shiel Ridge in Wester Ross. Now we repeated the traverse *and* crossed the deep passes at its end to add a Corbett and two more Munros. A ten-bagger. Even Allan found that tough.

Rain, snow, darkness... we carried on regardless, bolstered by a shared disposition to humour. On a day when the wind was measured at over 80mph on Cairn Gorm, we struggled to the summit of Creag Meagaidh, sheltered behind the cairn and couldn't make it back out again. After several attempts, we managed to crawl out along the frozen ground and slide down into the nearest corrie.

Sometimes we attempted too much. On the Isle of Arran, Allan's insistence on scrambling over every rocky nubbin on the Glen Rosa skyline, while I took the bypass path, resulted in us having to race back along Brodick seafront so as not to miss the ferry back to the mainland.

In the Cairngorms, we lingered too long on the Braeriach plateau and found ourselves disoriented in darkness without torches (don't ask) in the labyrinth of Rothiemurchus Forest. I have known others, in similar circumstances, succumb to rage, panic or mutual recrimination. Instead, our attempts to extricate ourselves by aiming for the location of a barking dog, which we assumed signified habitation, seemed so ridiculous that we merely succumbed to giggles. And yes, in case you're wondering, we did eventually surface at a roadside.

Then one Sunday morning in 2005, Sandi turned up on my doorstep to tell me Allan had been killed.

Although well-equipped, he had slipped while tackling a shortcut up a snow gully onto the summit ridge of Binnein Mor in the Mamores Range. He had hit a rock and punctured his skull.

I felt numb. Sandi felt numb. Later, as is the way of things, we cursed him for his foolhardiness, for his abandonment of us, for the senselessness of it all.

There was also guilt. I had been due to accompany him that weekend, before other commitments took precedence. Not for the first time, I might have been able to dissuade him from taking that shortcut. It was a thought on which I couldn't allow myself to dwell.

After the accident, conditions had become so dangerous that the Mountain Rescue team had been unable to reach him before darkness. Sandi was horrified that he'd had to remain up there overnight, in weather as atrocious as only the Scottish Highlands can muster. No, I said, seeking words of comfort for both of us. He'll love it. His last night, with the mountains all to himself. He won't even feel the cold.

Later, as is also sometimes the way of things, his girlfriend and best friend were drawn closer together in grief. Sandi and I became partners. I like to think Allan would approve. Sometimes on the hill, especially when the storm rages or my step falters, I hear him still, chuckling to himself at my discomfort, urging me ever onwards and upwards.

At his funeral service, they played his favourite song: 'Teenage Kicks' by The Undertones. It summed up his endless quest for adventure and experience. Too upset to speak at the service myself, I asked the Humanist Celebrant to read out Geoffrey Winthrop Young's classic poem 'I Hold The Heights'. It ends:

I may not grudge the little left undone,
I hold the heights, I keep the dreams I won.

Never had those evocative lines seemed so apt. Allan left us prematurely, but he had accomplished so much. There are worse epitaphs a man can have when the time comes.

49

Hillwalking Saved My Life

AS I STOOD at the summit of The Cairnwell in Glen Shee, surrounded by dull hillsides stripped of all definition by an overcast sky and polluted by the rusting machinery of downhill ski development, the Highlands had never looked so magnificent.

I'm not normally given to such flights of fancy. I don't

'conquer' mountains. I don't 'commune with nature'. I give short shrift to lazy clichés about 'spectacular scenery' and 'stunning views', and I cringe as I write 'magnificent'. But for once the word feels accurate. There may even have been a tear in my eye, though if you tell anyone I'll deny it.

But The Cairnwell? With a chairlift that takes couch potatoes to within a few hundred metres of the summit? I had always dismissed that particular mountain as one of the less interesting Munros.

This time was different. This time it was my first Munro following a heart attack six months earlier. It came out of the blue. I was fit and healthy – a guidebook writer, for goodness sake. This sort of thing didn't happen to someone like me. On the Sunday I'd climbed Ben Nevis to complete photography for a guidebook. On the Friday I was mee-mawed to hospital with chest pains and, one hour and one angioplasty later, I had two stents in my chest to unblock an artery.

In retrospect, there had been warning signs – I had been gasping my way up mountains for a couple of years and telling myself I couldn't expect to set personal bests forever. I put my survival down to a lifetime's hillwalking. My heart, strengthened from exercise, suffered only minor damage. As a former IT lecturer, I called the op my 'reboot'.

Of course, a heart attack does tend to put a dent in one's immediate hillwalking capabilities. Released from hospital after 48 hours, I walked down a flight of stairs and could barely make it back up again. A week later, on my first foray to a local coffee shop, I had to be driven home. It took me two weeks to walk round a nearby park without needing a rest.

As I live in Edinburgh, the first major goal I set myself was Arthur's Seat, the 251m landmark in the heart of the city. After three months I steeled myself to climb it, gingerly, scared to feel my heart pounding in my chest. At the summit, I felt not only relief but also a sense of achievement I haven't felt on mountains ten times as high.

During the next three months I graduated from Arthur's Seat

At the summit of Mount Elbert

to the Pentlands, the 500m range of hills on the outskirts of the city. Each time I survived, it increased my confidence, and so the time came for the next step: my first Munro.

When Sir Hugh Munro drew up his list of Scottish mountains in 1891, his figure of 3,000ft was a somewhat arbitrary cut-off point for distinguishing real mountains from also-rans. But now that invisible 3,000ft threshold assumed a concrete reality in my mind, representing both a physical and a psychological barrier.

The Cairnwell seemed a manageable objective, requiring only 270m of ascent from the Cairnwell Pass at its foot. Nevertheless, I tackled those 270m more tentatively than I had ever climbed any mountain in my life, with every sense greedy to affirm life. And I made it. I may not have 'conquered' the mountain, but I'd conquered my fear.

The euphoria lasted a whole two weeks, and then...

If there was a mantra drummed in to me by doctors and nurses it was this: *you can't rush things*. Recovery is stepwise, not linear, and I was about to take my first backward step. Two weeks after The Cairnwell, in a premature burst of over-confidence, I attempted three Munros on the opposite side of Glen Shee... and my heart refused to play ball. Even with the help of gravity, I barely made it down. I reached the car in a state of collapse.

A tad panicked by this, I consulted a local heart helpline. I was told that I'd simply overdone it and that *you cannot not damage the heart through exercise*. It was the reassurance I needed. The heart is a muscle. It merely needed building up further.

Fast forward a year and I was standing on top of Mount Elbert, a Colorado fourteener that at 14,440ft (4,404m) is the second highest mountain in the USA outside Alaska. It was a tough ascent, but that sort of altitude is always going to be tough for those of us who live at sea level. Not so long ago, I had been lying on a hospital bed. *Any* way I could climb to 4,000m was going to be okay by me.

At the summit, I thought of Percy Unna, the former President of the Scottish Mountaineering Club, whose generous donations enabled the National Trust for Scotland to purchase Glen Coe in 1935. After being diagnosed with a heart condition, he continued to climb alone so as not to cause distress to companions should he not make it back down. He died on the slopes of Stob Maol above Loch Awe in 1950.

Maybe that's how I'll go too. Or maybe I'll get knocked down by a bus. Who knows? My future is no more predictable than yours. I may not skip around the hills singing show tunes from *The Sound of Music*, but then I never did. What I can do, with a new lease of energy, is climb mountains more easily than I have for years.

And maybe, just maybe, I can be persuaded to try some of that communing with nature malarkey.

See you on the hill.

50

A Politically Correct
Hillwalking Fable

JACK AND JILL went up the hill, but not to fetch a pail of water. In common with the majority of UK households, their cohabitation had water on tap, and so they had no need for archaic methods of water procurement. In any case, there was no guarantee that water so obtained would have been uncontaminated by acid rain, industrial waste or other pollutants. No, the aim of Jack and Jill's pedestrian excursion had no hydrological motive whatsoever, indeed would be difficult to justify in a society geared to consumerist gain.

The objective of their ambulatory endeavour was simply to get to the top of the hill. This is not to imply that a summit is in any way a superior part of an eminence to any other part (except heightwise), nor that all foot travel should be goal-oriented, but simply to state that at this point in the space-time continuum, the summit was where they were going.

Although elevation criteria had played no part in their summit selection process, the hill Jack and Jill had chosen to ascend happened to be a Munro. They had originally intended to climb a non-Munro to avoid accusations of heightism, but after much deliberation they had come to the conclusion that to *not* climb a mountain simply because it was over 3,000ft high would open them to accusations of reverse heightism.

There was a path all the way to the summit, and it amused them to think that it followed a route once taken by Bonnie Prince Charlie, the original PC. In an ideal world, of course, it would be preferable for man (and woman) to leave no trace of his (or her) passing, but only an eco-fascist would ban a creature from the hill because its mode of locomotion caused soil compaction and ensuing path formation. Should the human race be held responsible for the process of natural selection that has given it its bipedal gait?

Jack and Jill debated whether to avoid the path in order to prevent further erosion, but they decided this might merely spread the disfigurement to flanking ecosystems and result in future incursive path re-engineering projects, which would further increase man's environmental impact. It was a difficult decision, but they concluded that the path was a natural phenomenon and they were morally justified in using it.

Their equipment evinced a similar environmental sensitivity. The dull sheen of their clothes, for example, was intended to diminish visual pollution and reduce disturbance to non-domesticated non-humans such as deer. Jill, guiltily surrendering to outmoded societal ideas of female attire, had originally intended to wear her colourful new top, but Jack had managed to bring her to her senses before any damage was done. Their inexpensive animal-hide boots troubled them, but they were too economically disadvantaged to afford lightweight synthetics with waterproof linings and eco-friendly soles. Similarly, they longed for the day they could afford to replace their woolly jumpers with technical fleece, and squirmed with guilt whenever they passed an ovine quadruped.

As a non-sexist pairing, each led the way in turn, with the follower assiduously avoiding the foot placements of the leader in order to diminish their combined impact on underfoot vegetation. At one point Jack unintentionally trampled on a flower and suffered several moments of intense internal debate concerning its revivification. While Jill simulated patience, he fashioned a splint from a small twig and attempted floral restoration. When this failed, he abandoned the flower to its fate, assuaging his conscience with the thought that it was not his place to impose human notions of order on Nature.

After this incident they settled into a pleasant upward rhythm that rendered them oblivious to further vegetative distractions. As they gained height they began to feel free of left-brain domination of thought, achieving a composure that could not even be disturbed by a series of unfortunate encounters – with a party of shouting schoolchildren shedding sherbet wrappers, a synchronised conga of charity walkers picking flowers, a pain of Munro baggers placing stones on superfluous cairns, and a gaggle of mountain rescuers playing with GPS navigational toys.

Jill especially became intensely attuned to her surroundings, so much so that, curiously energised by the phallic symbolism of a group of pinnacles, she forged ahead of Jack. Unaware of the true cause of her sudden surge, she mistakenly attributed her superior performance to the fact that Jack was more chronologically gifted, although she was too tactful to suggest he was past it. Equally mistakenly, Jack put her sudden spurt down to a carbohydrate-loaded breakfast. How she could put away those organic low-salt, low-sugar baked bean butties, he mused.

To replenish diminishing energy, Jack called for a lunch stop, and Jill reluctantly complied. Their core nutritional input consisted of slices of unrefined rye bread, spread thinly with low-fat non-hydrogenated vegetable margarine and strawberry compote, which in less sensitive times they had called jam sannies. These were followed by carob bars from a Brazilian co-operative, washed down with organic carrot juice.

After lunch they resumed their upward progress, but alas their renewed energy levels were to prove insufficient for the attainment of the summit. Taking a solitary step off the path to avoid a watery ecosystem, Jack tripped. This caused an imbalance of posture rapidly followed by a head-over-heels descent at a speed rarely achieved by primates. As he fell, Jack invaded Jill's personal space and precipitated a similar fall on her part. Thus Jack fell down, and Jill came tumbling after.

When they eventually came to a halt they found themselves incapable of voluntary lower body movement. Even more seriously, Jack had a large bump on his head. 'I think I've broke my crown,' he moaned.

Cognisant of his hypochondriac tendencies, Jill found her capacity for sympathy temporarily impaired. 'You're as optically challenged as a bat and as sanity impaired as a hatter,' she opined.

'I accept that I am to blame for our current immobilisation,' essayed Jack defensively, 'but my feet are no bigger than you would expect from the size of my skeletal frame.'

'They are veritable planks all the same,' said Jill, and immediately regretted her outburst. Had their relationship counsellor not told them to be more accommodating to each other's point of view? She offered an apology. Jack accepted unconditionally and would have reciprocated her concern with an enquiry after her own state of health, but he feared she might misconstrue this as an implication that she belonged to the weaker sex.

Jack was sure that the mountain rescue team had seen them fall, indeed imagined he had seen a grin on the face of the leader and mistakenly taken it as a signal of reassurance. But no one came to their aid. Perhaps it was more important for the team members to persevere with their training exercise, unimpeded by the distractions of Jack and Jill's situational reality, and Jack could understand this.

It began to snow, and their world turned white, enhancing the aesthetic attraction of their surroundings and giving the lie to colourist prejudices about picturesqueness. As time passed, they became increasingly thermally challenged and cerebrally constrained. And so our tale has a happy ending. The bodies of the alliterative couple finally became nonviable, their carcasses biodegraded, and their replenishing nutrients seeped into the thirsty soil of Mother Earth, who made herself ready for the next passing bipeds.

Some other books published by **LUATH** PRESS

The Joy of Hillwalking
Ralph Storer
ISBN 978-1-842820-69-8 PBK
£7.50

Hillwalking is only one of the passions in my life. In my experience, those who love the mountains are passionate people who are passionate about many things. That said, there are times, as I describe herein, when I simply have to go to the hills.

RALPH STORER

Ralph Storer's highly entertaining exploration of the lure of the hills is underpinned by hard-won experience – he has climbed extensively in the British Isles, Europe and the American West, though his abiding love is the Scottish Highlands. His breezy anecdotes of walking and climbing around the world in all sorts of conditions are gripping and full of fun. His sense of humour is as irrepressible as his relish for adventurous ascents, but he doesn't have his head in the clouds when it comes to serious issues such as public access and conservation.

A treat for all hillwalkers active or chairbound, as Ralph Storer... rambles over all aspects of enjoying and suffering, not only, Scottish, but he world's hills.
SCOTS INDEPENDENT

Having read and enjoyed Storer's previous books, it was a pleasure to receive a review copy of his latest work. A pleasure, and not a disappointment. Storer sets out to detail his modus walkaround in an interesting, none-too-serious round of seasons, summits, sex, etc.
THE ANGRY CORRIE

The Ultimate Guide to the Munros Volume 1: Southern Highlands

Ralph Storer
ISBN: 978-1-910021-58-3 PBK
£14.99

From the pen of a dedicated Munro bagger comes *The Ultimate Guide* to everything you've wished the other books had told you before you set off. The lowdown on the state of the path, advice on avoiding bogs and tricky situations, tips on how to determine which bump is actually the summit in misty weather... this is the only guide to the Munros you'll ever need.

This comprehensive rucksack guide to the Southern Highlands features:

- Detailed descriptions of all practicable ascent routes up all the Munros and Tops

- Easy to follow quality and difficulty ratings

- OS maps and colour photographs with marked routes

- The history of each Munro and Top

- Notes on technical difficulties, foul-weather concerns, winter conditions and scenery

... picks up where others – including my own – leave off.

CAMERON McNEISH

The Ultimate Guide to the Munros Volume 2: Central Highlands South

Ralph Storer
ISBN: 978-1-906817-20-6 PBK
£14.99

The Central Highlands region is the smallest of the six that constitute the Scottish Highlands and Islands, but it is packed with more Munros than any other. There are so many that *The Ultimate Guide to the Munros* series splits the region into two books: Volume 2 Central Highlands South and Volume 3 Central Highlands North.

Volume 2 covers the Munros south of Glen Nevis. It ranges from the scenic west coast mountains of Appin to the multi-Munro ridges of the Mamores. It also comprehensively covers the celebrated mountains of Glen Coe, including the startling arrowhead peak of Buachaille Etive Mor, the thrilling ridge of Aonach Eagach and the complex ridges and corries of Bidean nam Bian, the highest mountain in Argyll. With all the features that made Volume 1 so popular, Volumes 2 and 3 are a must for all Central Highlands hillwalkers.

Fabulously illustrated... Entertaining as well as informative... One of the definitive guides to the Munros.

PRESS AND JOURNAL

The Ultimate Guide to the Munros Volume 3: Central Highlands North

Ralph Storer
ISBN: 978-1-906817-56-5 PBK
£14.99

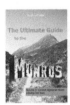

The Central Highlands region is the smallest of the six that constitute the Scottish Highlands and Islands, but it is packed with more Munros than any other. There are so many that *The Ultimate Guide to the Munros* series splits the region into two books: Volume 2 Central Highlands South and Volume 3 Central Highlands North.

Volume 3 begins with an extensive section on Ben Nevis, the 'King of All Munros', including multiple ascent routes as well as information on history, seasonal variations and safety considerations. From here, the guidebook ranges east over a great variety of mountain scenery to the more gentle Munros flanking Drumochter Pass on the A9. In the roadless country in between lie some of the most remote Munros in the Scottish Highlands, including majestic Ben Alder and the sky-high ridges of the Geal-Charn Group in the secret country around Loch Ericht.

With the winning combination of reliable advice and quirky humour, this is the ideal hillwalking companion.

SCOTS MAGAZINE

The Ultimate Guide to the Munros Volume 4: Cairngorms South

Ralph Storer
ISBN: 978-1-908373-51-9 PBK
£14.99

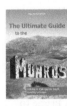

Volume 4 of *The Ultimate Guide to the Munros* extends the series to the Cairngorms National Park. As with the Central Highlands, the number and variety of ascent routes here is such that the region has been split into two books: Volume 4 Cairngorms South and Volume 5 Cairngorms North.

Volume 4 covers the area south of Deeside, where the crags of famed Lochnagar tower above Balmoral. In the nearby Glen Shee ski area south of Braemar are to be found some of the easiest Munros in the whole of the Highlands (made even easier by using a chairlift!), while in the wild country to their west lie some of the most awkward to reach.

As with other volumes in the series, this comprehensive rucksack guide makes extensive use of annotated photographs and OS maps and includes a wealth of other information that makes it a compelling hillwalking companion.

His books are exceptional... Storer subverts the guidebook genre completely.

THE ANGRY CORRIE

Baffies' Easy Munro Guide Volume 1: Southern Highlands

Ralph Storer
ISBN: 978-1-908373-08-3 PBK
£7.99

Baffies, the entertainments convenor of the Go-Take-a-Hike Mountaineering Club, is allergic to exertion, prone to lassitude, suffers from altitude sickness above 600m, blisters easily and bleeds readily. Think the Munros are too difficult? Think again. *Baffies' Easy Munro Guide* is the first of a series of reliable rucksack guides to some of the more easily tackled Munros.

Twenty-five routes, each covering one main Munro, all with detailed maps and full colour throughout – this lightly humorous and opinionated book will tell you everything you need to reach the summit. Thousands of people each year attempt to conquer the Munros. This friendly and accessible guide allows beginners and those looking for a less strenuous challenge to join in.

It is perfect for anyone exploring Scotland's beautiful mountains, whatever his or her level of experience.
GUIDEPOST

Baffies' Easy Munro Guide Volume 2: Central Highlands

Ralph Storer
ISBN: 978-1-908373205 PBK
£7.99

Think the Munros are too difficult? Think again.

Meet Baffies, the entertainments convenor of the Go-Take-a-Hike Mountaineering Club. Named after his footwear of choice [Baffies is a Scottish word for slippers], he is gifted in the art of finding the easiest way up any given mountain.

This is the second in the Baffies' Easy Munro Guide series of reliable rucksack guides to some of the more easily tackled Munros. Twenty-five routes, each covering one main Munro, all with detailed maps and full colour throughout – this lightly humorous and opinion-ated book will tell you everything you need to reach the summit.

Packed to bursting with concise information and route descriptions. There should be room for this guide in every couch potato's rucksack.
OUTDOOR WRITERS AND PHOTOGRAPHERS GUILD

... a truly outstanding guidebook.
UNDISCOVERED SCOTLAND

The Ultimate Mountain Trivia Quiz Challenge

Ralph Storer
ISBN: 978-1-908373-82-3 PBK
£7.99

Are you ready to tackle *The Ultimate Mountain Trivia Quiz Challenge?*

This is a quiz book for people who love the mountains and the outdoors. It will put your brain through its paces on a wide range of topics including the world's mountains, camping, weather, history, films… Add cryptic clues, anagrams and a whole pot pourri of teasers and twisters and there's something here for everyone.

The author of *100 Best Routes on Scottish Mountains* and *The Ultimate Guide to the Munros* series brings his quizzing skills and encyclopaedic knowledge of the outdoors to a book that will both inform and delight. Whether you're sitting by the campfire or in an armchair, the result is a thoroughly interesting and entertaining collection, as challenging as any mountain.

A thoroughly fascinating way to kill time – every bothy in the land should be furnished with a laminated copy, for those days when the wind comes up or the cloud comes down.

SCOTSMAN

50 Classic Routes on Scottish Mountains

Ralph Storer
ISBN: 978-1-842820-91-9 PBK
£6.99

Following on from *100 Best Routes on Scottish Mountains* and *50 Best Routes on Skye and Raasay*, this volume of 50 routes, updated from the hardback edition, completes a tour of Scotland that encompasses the best of Highlands and Islands hillwalking. Like its companion volumes, *50 Classic Routes* again ranges across the Highlands and Islands to provide an outstanding cross-section of routes, from gentle hillwalks to thrilling scrambles, from popular Munros to less well-known but equally rewarding mountains that will be a revelation even to those who think they know the Highlands well. All routes begin and end at the same place, are accessible by road and include a peak over 600m/2,000ft. Route descriptions are detailed yet concise, and each is accompanied by one of Ralph's helpful at-a-glance route grids, which give ratings for technical difficulty, terrain, seriousness and foul-weather navigatability. The book includes a map of each route and a selection of photographs. Let 50 Classic Routes help you make the most of your time in the Scottish mountains. Happy Walking!

Details of these and other books published by Luath Press can be found at: **www.luath.co.uk**

Luath Press Limited
committed to publishing well written books worth reading

LUATH PRESS takes its name from Robert Burns, whose little collie Luath (*Gael.,* swift or nimble) tripped up Jean Armour at a wedding and gave him the chance to speak to the woman who was to be his wife and the abiding love of his life.

Burns called one of 'The Twa Dogs' Luath after Cuchullin's hunting dog in Ossian's *Fingal*. Luath Press was established in 1981 in the heart of Burns country, and now resides a few steps up the road from Burns' first lodgings on Edinburgh's Royal Mile.

Luath offers you distinctive writing with a hint of unexpected pleasures.

Most bookshops in the UK, the US, Canada, Australia, New Zealand and parts of Europe either carry our books in stock or can order them for you. To order direct from us, please send a £sterling cheque, postal order, international money order or your credit card details (number, address of cardholder and expiry date) to us at the address below. Please add post and packing as follows: UK – £1.00 per delivery address; overseas surface mail – £2.50 per delivery address; overseas airmail – £3.50 for the first book to each delivery address, plus £1.00 for each additional book by airmail to the same address. If your order is a gift, we will happily enclose your card or message at no extra charge.

ILLUSTRATION: IAN KELLAS

Luath Press Limited
543/2 Castlehill
The Royal Mile
Edinburgh EH1 2ND
Scotland

Telephone: 0131 225 4326 (24 hours)
email: sales@luath.co.uk
Website: www.luath.co.uk